BITCOIN MINING DECODED

FROM CURIOSITY TO CONSULTANCY

SUNIL KUMAR
DUSAN MATUSKA

English (Indian)

Title: Bitcoin Mining Decoded : From curiosity to consultancy

Author: Dusan Matuska

ISBN: 978-81-988706-0-5

Published on: 03/06/2025

Published by:

In Association with

DIGITAL WRITOPRENEURS HUB AND ACADEMY, NEW DELHI

Mob: 91 72918 49502

About The Book

Bitcoin Mining Decoded is your ultimate guide to mastering the world of Bitcoin mining, whether you're just starting your journey or looking to deepen your expertise. Written by Bitcoin enthusiasts and industry leaders Sunil Kumar and Dusan Matuska, this book takes you through every step necessary to achieve mining success, from the basics to advanced consultancy and advisory services.

This comprehensive guide covers everything you need to know: from understanding the core principles of Bitcoin mining, blockchain and the intricacies of mining hardware, to the complexities of Bitcoin halvings, risk management, and legal and regulatory considerations. You'll also learn about building a successful Bitcoin mining business, offering consultancy services, and exploring the energy markets. All of these are essential components to thriving in this rapidly evolving industry.

What sets this book apart is its unique storytelling approach. Instead of feeling like a dry technical manual, Bitcoin Mining Decoded presents complex topics through an engaging narrative, making it accessible and enjoyable, even for those new to the subject. Whether you're a beginner just getting into Bitcoin or an experienced miner seeking fresh insights, this book provides valuable lessons and perspectives for everyone. By the time you finish reading, you'll be equipped with the knowledge and skills to navigate the world of Bitcoin mining with confidence, preparing you to become an expert ready to succeed in this exciting space.

Dive into this one-of-a-kind resource and discover how you can go from curiosity to consultancy, learning from real-world case studies and success stories along the way.

About The Author

Sunil Kumar

Sunil Kumar is a seasoned Mining Operations and Strategic Planning Manager at AmityAge, a passionate Blockchain Enthusiast, and a Certified Bitcoin Expert. He has over a decade of experience across the marine industry and the evolving world of Information Technology.

Born into a defence family, Sunil was raised with a strong sense of discipline and commitment. After completing his 12th standard, he joined the Merchant Navy at 17 and a half. After completing a diploma in Nautical Science, he began sailing by 18 and a half.

From 2012 to 2022, he had an extensive maritime career, sailing to 82 countries and working with 17 nationalities. He specialised in oil and chemical carriers, particularly oil tankers, often called "walking bombs". He completed a BSc in Nautical Science in 2016, followed by an MBA in Oil and Gas in 2018.

In 2018, Sunil's interest in Bitcoin mining began when a junior introduced him to the concept. He purchased his first miner and began learning, experimenting, and advising others. From 2018 to 2020, while pursuing a Postgraduate Programme in Data Science and Business Analytics, he also offered free consultancy to people across India.

During the Covid period, he explored Bitcoin mining professionally, travelling to Dubai, Abu Dhabi, and other regions. In 2022, he left sailing and briefly joined a French IT firm, consulting for a major FMCG company before launching his own IT business. He later shifted full focus to Bitcoin mining.

At BTC Prague in 2024, he met Dusan and began working with AmityAge. By December, he joined AmityAge as a Mining Operations and Strategy Planning Manager. Today, he is recognised as an expert in miner procurement, energy sourcing, and infrastructure planning.

He holds an Honorary Doctorate in Blockchain and Cryptocurrency Technology and is pursuing a Doctorate in Business and Analytics in the US, expected to finish in 2025. Through this book, Bitcoin Mining Decoded, he shares his journey to inspire others into the world of Bitcoin.

About The Author

Dusan Matuska

Dusan Matuska is a passionate Bitcoin Educator, Miner, and Advocate with a mission to welcome 100 million people into the world of Bitcoin. A lifelong educator at heart, Dusan began teaching mathematics, physics, and English at the age of 18, falling in love with the transformative power of education. This deep commitment to teaching has fuelled his journey into the world of Bitcoin, where he has dedicated himself to spreading knowledge about its potential to foster financial freedom.

Since getting deeper into Bitcoin in 2017, Dusan has become a leading voice in the Bitcoin community, organizing webinars, workshops, and academies to educate individuals about its impact. He is the host of the only Bitcoin-focused podcast in Slovak language, which has garnered over 150,000 listens, and he continues to inspire people to embrace Bitcoin's revolutionary potential.

In 2021, Dusan co-founded a Bitcoin mining operation in Slovakia, and by 2023, he and his colleague Gabriel became the largest Bitcoin miners in the Czech and Slovak region, managing a few thousands machines in Paraguay and Ethiopia. Their mining operations support global educational efforts, bringing Bitcoin's promise of financial empowerment to communities around the world.

In 2022, Dusan and his team set up the first Bitcoin Education Center in Honduras, on Roatán Island in the free private city of Próspera. There, they helped over 60 businesses adopt Bitcoin and educated hundreds of children about this transformative technology. Through his work, Dusan continues to push for wider Bitcoin adoption, empowering people to understand and participate in the future of money.

In Bitcoin Mining Decoded, Dusan shares his knowledge and experiences to help others navigate the exciting world of Bitcoin, hoping to inspire a new wave of global adoption.

Foreword

By Nico Smid

Since its launch in 2009, Bitcoin has evolved from a digital experiment into a globally recognized financial asset. As its value and influence have grown, Bitcoin mining has shifted from a hobbyist activity to a large-scale, industrial sector that draws increasing attention from governments and institutional investors. Modern mining operations are capital-intensive, highly competitive, and closely linked to global energy markets. As the industry matures, it's essential to understand how Bitcoin mining works, but for most people, the path into mining still feels intimidating, full of jargon, volatility, and a closed knit community.

That's why this book matters.

Bitcoin Mining Decoded is a clear, grounded, and more important human guide to the mining world, from the first spark of curiosity to building a career as a consultant in this space. Sunil Kumar and Dusan Matuska have written a unique story. It is technical but at the same time takes you on an international journey.

This book isn't just about how mining works. It's about how people work their way into it. It shows you the real-world decisions, mistakes, setups, trade-offs, and breakthroughs. You'll learn about ASICs and energy markets. But you'll also learn how a sailor became a miner, how an educator became an operator, and how curiosity can turn into a calling.

If you're just getting started in Bitcoin mining, this book will save you time and confusion. If you've been around the block and want to go deeper there's a ton of value here too.

Sunil and Dusan have walked the walk. I've seen their work in the mining industry up close, and I know this book comes from lived experience, not theory.

Read it. Learn from it. And maybe, like the authors, you'll find yourself not just mining Bitcoin, but mining meaning, purpose, and opportunity in one of the most exciting industries of our time.

Enjoy the journey from curiosity to consultancy.

Nico Smid
Founder, Digital Mining Solutions

Foreword

By Dr. Khushboo Khullar

In recent years, Bitcoin mining has evolved from a niche technical pursuit into a global industry that shapes energy markets, drives technological innovation, and underpins the monetary infrastructure of the world's most decentralized digital asset. Despite its growing significance, mining is still poorly understood outside a small circle of insiders. To most, it feels intimidating, opaque, or too technical to even begin exploring.

That's precisely why Bitcoin Mining Decoded is such a timely and important book.

Authors Sunil Kumar and Dusan Matuska have crafted something truly distinctive. This isn't your typical mining whitepaper, nor is it a dry technical handbook that leaves non-engineers scrambling for Google. What sets this book apart is its unique storytelling approach. You'll find yourself drawn in by the narrative—hooked by the simplicity, the analogies, and the way it demystifies the most complex concepts. It's accessible and enjoyable, even for those brand new to Bitcoin. And yet, for the pros? There's real depth. Whether you're a beginner just plugging in your first rig, or a seasoned operator navigating geopolitical risk, this book will level you up.

The theme of the book also resonates deeply with my own academic and professional journey. My PhD thesis in energy security explored how decentralized systems like Bitcoin mining can actually stabilize power grids—by tapping stranded energy and incentivizing renewables.

Having transitioned from traditional finance to working directly with Bitcoin-native entrepreneurs, I particularly value the authors' treatment of mining's intersection with capital markets. One major trend to watch? Bitcoin-backed loans. Increasingly, industrial miners are using their Bitcoin holdings as collateral to secure working capital—addressing the volatility and high upfront costs of the business. The smartest operators today are more than engineers—they're strategic CFOs- optimizing liquidity, managing credit, and building durable businesses.

Bitcoin Mining Decoded captures that evolution. It's a rare blend of hashrate and heart—technical where it needs to be, but always human at its core.

Whether you're a curious learner, a startup founder, an investor looking for signal in the noise, or just someone trying to make sense of the buzz around mining—this book belongs on your shelf. Read it, share it, and keep it close.

Here's to more nodes, more hashrate, and fewer question marks.

Dr. Khushboo Khullar
Venture Partner, Lightning Ventures

Acknowledgements

By Sunil Kumar

Writing Bitcoin Mining Decoded: From Curiosity to Consultancy has been one of the most transformative journeys of my life. This book is not just a product of research, hard work, and sleepless nights but also a labor of love, sacrifice, and unwavering support from the most important people in my life.

First and foremost, I extend my deepest thanks to my wife, Mamta—the true Ministry of Home Affairs in my life. She was my anchor and my greatest supporter when I took the bold step of leaving behind a decade-long career as a merchant marine where I had already risen to a higher rank. She has sacrificed so much to allow me to follow my dreams, and her unwavering presence kept my ship steady even in the roughest seas. As a homemaker, she made sure that I not only pursued my goals but did so with focus, determination, and a home filled with love. Mamta, you've been an anchor that doesn't drag but holds everything in place.

To my parents, Rajpal Singh and Sunita Ralia, words cannot express the gratitude I feel for you. You've supported me unconditionally at every step, even when Bitcoin and its ecosystem were alien concepts. Your faith in me has been the steady moor to my ship, keeping me grounded and reminding me of the strength I carry because of my roots.

A special thanks to Dusan and the entire team at Amity Age. Meeting Dusan was one of the pivotal moments in my Bitcoin journey. It merely took me five minutes of speaking with him to know that I wanted to work alongside him. Joining AmityAge meant leaving behind a self-branded consultancy that I had successfully built, but it was a decision I have never once doubted. The business ethics, the sheer dedication to educating others about Bitcoin, and the freedom and trust the team gives me to lead strategic planning and R&D without questions have fueled my passion and purpose in ways I cannot describe. This book is a reflection of everything we've worked on together, and I am grateful to each of you for inspiring and empowering me.

To Hanuman, my friend, my mentor, and my spiritual guide—you've been a constant source of blessings and positivity. As the Hindu god who personifies strength, devotion, and loyalty, you've always ensured that I have the energy and good vibes to accomplish my goals. I'm eternally blessed to have your presence and guidance in my life.

This book is not just for Bitcoin enthusiasts or professionals; it's for creators, innovators, and anyone who dreams of building something extraordinary. To the readers holding this book, you are now part of this journey too. I hope you feel the passion in its pages, the lessons it carries, and the energy of the people who inspired it.

For every sleepless night, roadblock, and doubt I overcame, I owe it to the extraordinary people who have stood by me. This book is for them, and it is for you, the readers, who are on your own journey to shape the future with your vision.

Thank you for being part of this adventure, and welcome aboard.

Sunil Kumar

Acknowledgements

By Dušan Matuška

Writing Bitcoin Mining Decoded has been an extraordinary journey, one that would not have been possible without the inspiration, support, and contributions of many incredible people along the way.

First and foremost, I want to extend my deepest thanks to **Sunil Kumar**, my colleague and co-sailor on this project. It was Sunil's idea to write this book—to open the doors of Bitcoin mining to those curious, eager, and ready to dive in. His tireless work, deep technical knowledge, and strategic vision brought structure and clarity to every chapter. Sunil, your passion for Bitcoin and dedication to helping others understand it has left a powerful imprint on these pages.

I want to express my deep gratitude to **Gabriel**, my business partner and brother-in-arms in the world of mining. While I was already immersed in Bitcoin, it was Gabriel who, in 2021, challenged me to take the leap into Bitcoin mining. His boldness and entrepreneurial spirit helped us scale from a local setup to running thousands of machines across Paraguay and Ethiopia. Without his push, none of this would exist at the scale it does today.

A heartfelt thank you to the **Paralelná Polis** community in Bratislava, and to the many cypherpunks whose questions, skepticism, and curiosity pushed me to think deeper. The countless Bitcoiners I've had the pleasure of speaking with—each conversation helped refine the ideas shared in this book.

And finally, thank you to all the **technical minds** who stood beside me during the long nights of problem-solving and innovation. Your work turned theory into practice.

This book is for all of you.
With deep appreciation,
Dušan Matuška

Prologue

Into the Engine Room of Bitcoin

Money has always been at the center of human cooperation. From shells and salt to gold and paper, every version of money has served as a tool to store value and coordinate effort. But with time, these tools have been bent, inflated, and often broken by those in control of their issuance.

Bitcoin is different. It's not here to play by the old rules—it rewrites them entirely. By anchoring itself in code, mathematics, and energy, Bitcoin offers a new foundation. A foundation where scarcity isn't a promise—it's enforced. Where value isn't printed—it's earned. And at the heart of it all lies a process that is often misunderstood, yet absolutely critical: mining.

If Bitcoin is the hardest money the world has ever seen, then mining is the furnace in which that hardness is forged. It is what gives Bitcoin its resistance to manipulation, censorship, and decay. It is the process that transforms raw electricity into incorruptible truth.

This book won't spend pages explaining what Bitcoin is—that's been done well elsewhere. Instead, we'll go deeper into how Bitcoin survives and why mining is the mechanism that keeps it alive. Whether you're a curious beginner or an industry practitioner, you'll find both the fundamentals and the nuances here—from plugging in your first machine, to designing scalable operations, to consulting others with confidence.

Together with my colleague Sunil Kumar, whose deep operational knowledge and strategic perspective have shaped much of this work, we've built this guide to help you move from theory to action.

This book is your entry point into the engine room of Bitcoin. So grab your curiosity—and maybe some earplugs—and step inside. It's time to decode Bitcoin mining.

Let's begin.

- **Sunil Kumar & Dusan Matuska**

Contents

CHAPTER 1
INTRODUCTION TO BITCOIN

One day, there was an epic event in Prague, the Bitcoin Capital of Europe, called BTC Prague. Sunil was invited there from India as a guest by his friend Dusan.

There is actually an interesting backstory to this meeting. Sunil was a sailor all life, and he had once been told about Bitcoin by one of his juniors while sailing. This generated curiosity and Sunil started researching all information available online about Bitcoin. This is how he came across Dusan on LinkedIn, and decided to connect with him. Dusan is a widely known Bitcoin educator and consultant. He started to eagerly ask him all sorts of questions to learn more about Bitcoin, and that is how Dusan ended up inviting Sunil to the event at Prague!

The conference centre buzzed with energy as thousands of Bitcoin enthusiasts moved between colourful booths and packed presentation halls. BTC Prague was turning out to be even bigger than anyone expected, with attendees from over fifty countries filling the venue. Bright orange Bitcoin logos adorned everything from t-shirts to coffee mugs, while screens displayed videos from various Bitcoin circular economies or slides with interesting mining statistics.

"Dusan, you have been a Bitcoin miner for such a long time. And you're doing so well! Tell me more." Sunil leaned forward, his young face eager and curious. At twenty-nine, he still had the restless energy that made him a good sailor, but right now he was on break and hunting for new opportunities. When Dusan had invited him to Prague, he'd thought: *Why not?*

Dusan, only thirty himself but already establishing a name in the Bitcoin world, grinned as he pushed his laptop aside. "It's simple and really interesting. I'll explain!" The excitement in his voice was contagious. "See, when money is easy to make, society begins to break. Well, probably the only solution we have, is Bitcoin."

He gestured to the bustling conference around them. "These people get it. There are CEOs, developers, and even some government officials here. All trying to understand what we already know!"

Dusan ran a hand through his short dark hair, a habit he'd picked up since leaving his sailor days behind just three years ago. "Back in 2008, this guy Satoshi Nakamoto became fed up with government money, with all the corruption, the manipulation, and all the fuss. So he created a digital currency, digital money that can be sent directly from one person to another without any bank or government involved."

He tapped his coconut water can for emphasis. "And the best part? It's hard money! Bitcoin is very hard to make more of. Each new coin gets added to the supply only after a computer works its butt off to solve a math problem where there's no shortcut. And solving it costs a ton of energy and time."

Sunil's eyes darted to a nearby group taking selfies with a life-sized Bitcoin mascot - Honeybadger. "Okay, but if it's on a computer, can't a hacker just copy and paste it? Duplicate it?" He mimicked typing on a keyboard.

Dusan laughed. "Not with Bitcoin! You have a public record of every bitcoin ever created. It's called the blockchain. It's like a massive puzzle, and each bitcoin has its own unique shape!" He pulled out his phone to show Sunil a blockchain explorer app called Mempool.space. "And because everyone has a copy of this public record, if someone tries to fake a bitcoin, it won't fit the puzzle and will get kicked out by the network before anyone can use it!" He lowered his voice even as a cheer erupted from a nearby presentation. "That's why Bitcoin is so safe from criminals and the government..."

"Wow!" Sunil's eyes widened as he watched dozens of transactions appear on Dusan's screen in real-time. "That is really interesting..." Behind them, a woman was explaining mining rigs to an attentive crowd. "But if it's so good, everyone will start using it, and then we'll have inflation, right?"

Dusan shook his head confidently. "Dollars and other government currencies can be printed endlessly; like, literally without stopping. But there will only ever be 21 million bitcoin. Ever. It's almost impossible to inflate." He pointed to a digital counter on a massive screen showing the current Bitcoin supply. "The only way to get it is to earn it or buy it from someone who already has it."

Sunil ran his fingers through his curly black hair, scepticism flashing across his face. "No offense, but if someone is controlling the coin, couldn't they manipulate it just like the government?"

"Nobody controls it!" Dusan's voice rose above the ambient noise of the conference. "That's the beauty! Not a single person does. It's controlled by a public network of Bitcoin users that anyone can join. So if someone wanted to change something in Bitcoin's code, they would need to convince every one of the millions of Bitcoin users to agree to it." He gestured around the packed hall. "Just look at all these different people. Otherwise, the change doesn't happen. And when has almost everybody of us agreed on anything?"

"Touché," Sunil grinned as they navigated through a crowd gathering for the next speaker. "Wow, I didn't know made-up money could make so much sense..."

Dusan grabbed two fresh coconut drinks from a passing tray. "Today, millions of people send bitcoin instantly and cheaply to each other around the world without any bank or government involved. And because bitcoin is hard money, you can't just print more of it. The more people who use it, the more valuable it becomes!"

He pointed toward the main stage where a famous Bitcoin advocate was about to speak to a standing-room-only crowd. "I'm not saying that Bitcoin will make you rich quick or overnight. Right now, only about one percent of the world owns bitcoin, and because it's still being adopted, some days it goes up and some days, yeah, even down." He raised an eyebrow. "Also, investments that are potentially lucrative can be risky."

"Oh, I think I get it," Sunil nodded, his expression brightening as they joined the crowd for the keynote. "Good money should be easy to use but hard to create. And because Bitcoin is digital, it's fast and cheap to use! And the blockchain with the proof of work mechanism makes it hard to inflate!" He bumped Dusan's shoulder with his own. "Perfect... thanks Dusan!"

As they turned their attention to the stage, Sunil couldn't help but wonder if his sailing break might turn into something more permanent. After all, there seemed to be some interesting waves to ride in this Bitcoin world.

CHAPTER 2
UNDERSTANDING BLOCKCHAIN

The morning sessions had just wrapped up, and BTC Prague was absolutely nuts. People everywhere. The exhibition hall was this crazy maze of booths with all kinds of Bitcoin stuff, ranging from hardware wallets, mining rigs, you name it. Sunil was trying his best to keep up with Dusan as they pushed through the crowd. Every few steps, Dusan would grab some free sticker or stop to watch someone demonstrating something.

"Dude, I had no clue this would be such a big deal," Sunil said, sidestepping a bunch of guys taking selfies with someone Dusan had pointed out as some kind of "Bitcoin celebrity", whoever that was. "Like, on the ship, I'd just hear random stuff about Bitcoin and crypto from guys checking their phones when we were supposed to be working."

Dusan laughed. "Yeah man, that's exactly how I started! Using my trading skills I got on forex when I was 17 to trade some crypto. But then I kind of fell down the rabbit hole philosophically and..." he suddenly stopped mid-sentence, his attention caught by something else. "Oh wonderful, they're about to start lunch in the main hall. I'm starving. Let's go grab something before the afternoon talks."

They pushed their way to the conference centre's restaurant, which the organizers had decked out with all this Bitcoin stuff. The menu even had these cheesy names like "Satoshi's Special" and "Blockchain Burger." The place was packed as hell, but they managed to find a tiny table in the corner after hovering awkwardly for a few minutes.

"Get the goulash," Dusan said, pointing at the menu. "Czech goulash is a killer."

When their food finally showed up, Sunil took a spoonful. "Damn, this is good. And this whole place is just... wow. First Bitcoin thing I've ever been to and it's truly blowing my mind."

"First time learning about Bitcoin at all, pretty much," he added, dipping his spoon to goulash again. "You've explained some basics, and I sort of get it, but there's still a ton I don't understand."

"Like what?" Dusan asked with his mouth half-full of bread.

Sunil took a swig of beer. "OK so you mentioned this blockchain thing. You said it's like some public record thing, but I still don't really get what the hell it actually is or how it works."

Dusan wiped his mouth. "Oh perfect. I was hoping to get into all that blockchain and mining stuff with you today." He grabbed a handful of napkins and dug around in his pocket for a pen. "Check this out. I'll show you what blockchain is."

He started scribbling on one of the napkins. "So remember when I said Bitcoin has this public record of every transaction ever? That's the blockchain. It's basically just a chain of blocks. That's literally where the name comes from, and each block has a bunch of transactions in it."

He drew a bunch of connected squares. "Think of each block like a page in a notebook. When the page gets filled up with all these transaction records, we seal it shut and add it to the book. Then we start a fresh page."

Sunil nodded slowly. "OK but who's in charge of this notebook? You said nobody controls Bitcoin."

"That's the clever part," Dusan said, grabbing another napkin because he'd already filled the first one. "The ledger gets maintained by everyone running the Bitcoin software. Thousands of computers all over the world all have a copy of the entire blockchain."

"The whole thing?" Sunil raised his eyebrows. "How big is it?"

"Hundreds of gigs now," Dusan said between bites. "But regular people don't need the whole blockchain to use Bitcoin. You can run simplified versions. It's the miners and nodes who keep the complete thing."

"Miners? Like, gold miners?" Sunil looked confused again.

Dusan snorted. "Kind of! But instead of digging for gold, Bitcoin miners are just solving math problems with computers." He jabbed at his napkin drawing. "Their job is basically to check transactions first and order them by adding new blocks to the blockchain."

A server came by and refilled their drinks. Dusan waited till she walked away before continuing.

"So here's how it works," he said, drawing more stuff on the napkin. "Say you make a Bitcoin transaction, like sending some bitcoin to me. That transaction gets broadcast to the network. Miners grab a bunch of transactions and put them in a block."

"But they can't just slap the block onto the blockchain right away," he continued. "They have to solve this puzzle first. This super hard math problem that needs tons of computing power."

"What kind of problem?" Sunil asked with his mouth full.

"It's called a hash function," Dusan explained. "Basically, miners have to find this special number that, when you mix it with the block data and run it through an algorithm, gives a result that fits certain rules."

Seeing Sunil's eyes glazing over, Dusan back pedalled. "OK, way simpler version. Imagine you've got this magic box. You stick all the transaction data in it, plus some random number. When you close the box and shake it, it spits out this long string of letters and numbers. The miners are trying different random numbers to find one that makes the output string start with a certain pattern, like a bunch of zeros."

"And that's hard because...?" Sunil asked.

"Because there's no shortcut to figuring out what number will work," Dusan said. "You just have to try trillions of different numbers until you find one that works. It's like playing the lottery."

"That sounds... really inefficient," Sunil said.

Dusan nodded. "It's supposed to be! That's the whole point. They call it 'Proof of Work' because miners have to prove they did a ton of computational work to add a block. That's what makes the Bitcoin blockchain secure. It also helps people running Bitcoin software to agree on, which version of the blockchain is the correct one. In order to mess with it, you'd need more computing power than everyone else combined."

They both shut up for a minute while they continued working on their goulash. The restaurant was noisy as a thrift market, with people yammering away in languages from all over the world.

"So these miners," Sunil said, wiping his mouth, "they do all this work just to... what? Add a page to the book?"

"They get paid," Dusan explained. "Two ways: First, they get fees from all the transactions in their block. Second, and the big one, each new block creates brand new bitcoin. Right now it's 3.125 bitcoin, which goes to whoever mined the block."

"That's how new bitcoin gets released," he added. "Not printed by some bank or government. It's created through mining."

Sunil swirled his beer thoughtfully. "And this happens... how often?"

"A new block gets added approximately every ten minutes," Dusan said. "The system automatically tweaks how hard the mining puzzle is to keep that rate steady, no matter how many miners join or how fancy their equipment gets."

"Huh," Sunil said. "So the blockchain is this never-ending record of all Bitcoin transactions, maintained by these miners competing to add new blocks."

"Exactly!" Dusan grinned. "And since everyone's got a copy, and each block is mathematically linked to the one before it, you can't really change past transactions. If you try to mess with something in an earlier block, it breaks all the math connections, and everyone sees you're tampering with it."

As they were finishing up lunch, the PA system crackled to life announcing the afternoon keynote in fifteen minutes.

"Oh we should definitely catch this one," Dusan said, checking his phone. "It’s a session about different blockchain types. Super relevant to what we've been talking about."

They headed to the main hall, which was filling up fast. They found seats somewhere in the middle as the lights dimmed and a woman in a business suit walked onstage.

"Good afternoon, everyone," she began confidently. "Today I want to talk about something pretty fundamental: not all blockchains are created equal."

The screen behind her showed a diagram with three different blockchain types.

"Most people think of blockchain like Bitcoin's model. Public, permissionless, where anyone can participate, see the ledger, and potentially become a miner. But that's just one type."

She pointed to the first part of her diagram. "Public blockchains like Bitcoin are decentralized, transparent, and open to all. No single entity runs the show, which makes them resistant to censorship and corruption."

Moving to the second section, she continued, "Private blockchains work within a single organization. The organization controls who can read the blockchain, submit transactions, and participate in consensus. These are good for internal record-keeping and auditing."

The final section highlighted consortium blockchains. "These are somewhere in the middle. They're run by a group of organizations rather than one entity or the public. For example, a bunch of banks might run a consortium blockchain for settlement processes."

Sunil leaned over to Dusan. "So Bitcoin uses the public one, right?"

Dusan nodded. "Yes. That's what makes it so game-changing. Anyone can join, use it, or help maintain it."

As the lady continued, she got into the technical differences between these blockchain types. "Public blockchains typically use mechanisms like Proof of Work when participants don't trust each other. Private blockchains can use simpler mechanisms since all participants are pre-verified."

She clicked a slide showing performance comparisons. "This is the classic blockchain trilemma. You can optimize for security, decentralization, or scalability, but it's really hard to max out all three. Bitcoin prioritizes security and decentralization over transaction speed. Scaling and speed gets solved on the second layers like Lightning Network."

And that is how Sunil got his first correct induction to the blockchain technology. And he was so intrigued by the new world he was experiencing today, that he simply couldn't wait to learn more. Luckily, he had Dusan to take him to the next chapter of this journey.

CHAPTER 3

BITCOIN MINING BASICS

After the keynote, everyone split up into smaller workshops. Dusan grabbed Sunil's shoulder. "Come on, there's a mining demo happening. You have to see this."

They walked up to this super loud booth where a bunch of computers were running, fans blasting so loud they could barely hear each other.

"These are ASIC miners," Dusan half-shouted over the noise. "Application-Specific Integrated Circuits. They're specially designed just for Bitcoin mining and nothing else."

Sunil looked at the machines. "They're sort of ugly."

"They don't need to be pretty," laughed the woman running the booth, who had blue streaks in her hair. "They just need to be efficient. Each one of these bad boys is like thousands of times better at mining than a regular computer."

"And hot as hell," Dusan added, feeling the warm air blasting from the fans. "That's why a lot of mining happens in places where the temperatures are friendly, like Finland, Iceland, Norway, US, Ethiopia, Russia, China, etc. Cold weather helps with cooling, plus some places have dirt-cheap electricity from coal, geothermal or water."

The woman nodded. "Power cost is the big factor in mining profitability. That's why mining operations cluster in places with cheap electricity."

As they walked away from the noisy booth, Sunil looked a bit overwhelmed. They found a quieter spot by a coffee stand.

"Let me see if I've got this straight," Sunil said as they waited for their coffees. "Miners are basically racing to solve some math puzzle. Whoever solves it first gets to add the next block and gets some fresh bitcoin as a reward."

"Plus transaction fees," Dusan reminded him. "Don't forget those."

"Right," Sunil continued. "And the blockchain is this distributed ledger that records all Bitcoin transactions, with copies on thousands of computers all over the world so nobody can mess with it."

"You got it," Dusan said, looking pleased. "The system is fool proof, meaning you don't have to trust any specific person or institution. You just “trust” but mainly you can verify the math and the protocol."

Their coffees showed up, and Dusan took a grateful gulp before continuing.

"So let me walk you through how a Bitcoin transaction actually works," he said. "Say you want to send me one bitcoin. First, you need a Bitcoin wallet."

Dusan smirked. "Which isn't really a wallet."

"No?" Sunil raised an eyebrow.

"Nah," Dusan chuckled. "It doesn't 'hold' your Bitcoin like a real wallet holds cash. It holds your private keys, which are basically secret passwords that prove you can spend a certain bitcoin."

"So where are the actual bitcoins?" Sunil asked.

"They exist as records on the blockchain," Dusan explained. "Your wallet just gives you the ability to control them. When you 'send' bitcoin, you're really just updating the blockchain to show that those bitcoins now belong to someone else."

He pulled out his phone and opened a wallet app. "Check it out. This is my Bitcoin address. It is kind of like a bank account number, except anyone can see it." He showed Sunil a string of letters and numbers. "If you wanted to send me bitcoin, you'd punch this address into your wallet."

"Then what happens?" Sunil asked.

"Your wallet creates a transaction message that says something like 'Transfer one bitcoin from Sunil's address to Dusan's address.' This message gets digitally signed using your private key, which proves you authorized it."

Dusan continued, "That signed transaction gets broadcast to the Bitcoin network, which are all those computers running the Bitcoin software. Miners grab it and include it in the block they're working on."

"Eventually, some miner solves the proof-of-work puzzle and adds their block with your transaction in it, to the blockchain," he said. "At that point, the transfer is confirmed, and I can spend the bitcoin you sent me."

Sunil frowned. "How long does all that take?"

"About ten minutes on average for the first confirmation depending on the fee you paid," Dusan said. "Though for big transactions, people usually wait for multiple confirmations to be extra sure. Each confirmation is another block added on top, making it even more secure."

"That doesn't seem too fast," Sunil pointed out. "My bank transfers are quicker."

"True," Dusan acknowledged. "But your bank can also freeze your account, block your transaction, or reverse it later. And international transfers? Those take forever and cost a fortune. With Bitcoin, nobody can stop or reverse your transaction, and it works exactly the same whether you're sending money across the table or across the world."

They finished their coffees and headed back into the main hall, where a panel discussion with miners from different countries was happening.

A woman from Kazakhstan was talking about her mining operation. "We've set up near hydroelectric dams that produce too much electricity during certain seasons. Instead of that energy going to waste, we use it for mining."

Next, a guy from Texas grabbed the mic. "Our operation actually helps stabilize the power grid. When electricity demand spikes, we can shut down immediately, freeing up power for homes and businesses. We've got deals with the grid operator that work for both of us."

Dusan nodded along. "That's another cool thing. Mining is super flexible with power consumption. It can use up electricity that would otherwise just go to waste."

As the panel kept going, Sunil found himself fascinated by all the technical challenges the miners described. They ranged from dealing with heat to tweaking equipment performance to handling market ups and downs.

After the panel wrapped up, they decided to take a break from all the technical stuff. They jumped in a taxi and drove a few kilometres to the city centre. They found a small terrace overlooking the Vltava river, with Prague Castle off in the distance.

"Beautiful city," Sunil said, taking in the view.

"For real," Dusan agreed. "Perfect mix of old and new. Kind of like what we're doing with money."

They hung out on the terrace, enjoying the breeze and the break from the conference chaos.

"So, after everything you've heard today, what do you think?" Dusan asked.

Sunil thought for a moment. "It's cool tech. I see why you are so into this. But I'm still wrapping my head around some stuff."

"Like what?"

"Well, this proof of work thing seems a bit... wasteful? All that electricity just to update a ledger?"

Dusan nodded thoughtfully. "Yeah, I get that criticism. I thought the same initially. But think about what it's replacing. The entire banking system with all its buildings, employees, armoured trucks, vaults, and servers. When you add up all the resources that system burns through, Bitcoin starts to look pretty efficient. Plus when a new Bitcoin block is mined, those transactions included inside of it will only need a tiny amount of electricity to be used to verify them by the

Bitcoin participants. They will not need any more “wasteful” mining energy in future. It is done only once per each transaction."

"I hadn't thought of it that way," Sunil admitted.

"Plus," Dusan continued, "the energy use serves a purpose. It's what makes Bitcoin secure and tamper-proof. Without proof of work, we'd be back to relying on trusted middlemen. That is exactly what Bitcoin was designed to get rid of."

They watched a tour boat cruise lazily down the river.

"Another thing," Sunil said after a while. "If mining gets harder as more miners join, won't it eventually become impossible?"

"Not impossible, just more competitive," Dusan explained. "The difficulty adjusts to keep that ten-minute block time. But yeah, you're right that small miners are finding it tougher to compete with these massive mining farms."

"So much for decentralization," Sunil remarked.

"Still way more decentralized than traditional banking," Dusan countered. "Plus, there are mining pools where smaller miners can team up and share rewards.

They fell silent for a bit, just enjoying the view. In the distance, church bells rang out the hour.

"You know what," Sunil said eventually, "when you first invited me to this thing, I figured it would be super boring technical stuff. But it's actually pretty cool to see all these people building something totally new."

Dusan smiled. "That's exactly what hooked me in. It's not just about the tech or even the money. It's about creating a different kind of financial system. One that's open to everyone, resistant to censorship, and not controlled by the usual power players."

"I think I'm starting to get it," Sunil said. "Bitcoin isn't just digital money; it's a whole different way of thinking about how we move and store value."

"Bingo," Dusan replied, clapping him on the shoulder. "Now you're seeing the big picture."

They stood in comfortable silence for another minute before Dusan checked his phone.

"We should probably head back in. There's a session on global adoption starting soon. I think you'll really enjoy it. There will be lots of stories about how Bitcoin is being used in countries where the local currency is going to shit."

As they drove back toward the conference hall, Sunil had one more question.

"With everything you've told me about blockchain and mining, I'm curious how did you actually get started? Seems like there's a pretty steep learning curve."

Dusan laughed. "Oh man, I made a ton of mistakes at first. Lost some money, stayed up way too many nights reading technical notes. But that's a whole other story, I'll tell you over dinner tonight. There's this awesome Czech restaurant near our hotel that has the best svíčková you'll ever taste."

Sunil grinned. "I'm holding you to that. Both the story and the food."

They re-joined the crowd heading back into the main hall for the next session. For Sunil, what had started as just visiting a friend was turning into an eye-opening journey into a world he never knew existed. A world that, despite all its complexity, offered a pretty simple promise: financial freedom for anyone willing to learn the rules.

CHAPTER 4
THE TECHNOLOGY BEHIND BITCOIN MINING

By the time Sunil and Dusan left the conference centre, the sun was setting over Prague's skyline, painting the old buildings with warm orange light. They'd spent the whole day bouncing between talks, demos, and chatting with random Bitcoin enthusiasts from all over the world. Sunil's head was buzzing with information overload.

"Man, I'm starving," Dusan said as they walked along the cobblestone streets, dodging tourists taking photos of the historic architecture. "That restaurant I told you about is just around the corner. Best traditional Czech food in the city, I promise."

"Thank god," Sunil replied. "My brain needs a break and my stomach needs filling."

The restaurant was tucked away on a narrow side street, the kind of place tourists would walk right past. Inside, it was warm and cosy with dark wooden beams across the ceiling, old farming tools hanging on the walls, and the mouth-watering smell of roasted meat filling the air. Most of the tables were already packed with locals.

"Dobrý večer!", the host greeted them. Dusan responded with something in Czech or Slovak that made the man laugh and slap him on the back.

"What did you say to him?" Sunil asked as they were led to a corner table.

"I told him we need lots of food and beer because I've been talking about Bitcoin all day and my friend's brain is melting," Dusan grinned. "I've been coming here, since I visit Prague often. They know me."

They settled in and ordered beers, which arrived quickly in massive mugs. Dusan took a long gulp and let out a satisfied "Ahh."

"OK so you promised me two things," Sunil said, after taking a sip of his own beer. "That amazing food you've been hyping up, and the story of how you got into Bitcoin mining."

"Food's coming," Dusan said, gesturing to the waiter who was already heading their way with steaming plates. "And yeah, I'll tell you my story. But first, let's eat. I'm really starving."

The waiter set down plates of svíčková. That's tender beef in a creamy sauce with dumplings, along with some other dishes Dusan had ordered for them to share.

"Amazing food, this is good," Sunil said after his first bite. For a few minutes, they just ate in hungry silence.

"Alright," Dusan finally said, pushing his empty plate away. "So you wanted to know how I got into mining?"

"Yeah. After everything you explained today, it sounds complicated as hell. How'd you figure it all out?"

Dusan leaned back in his chair, another beer already in hand. "So when I was still sailing in 2017, I met with my friend Peter. I asked him what he was doing during the last few months we haven't seen each other. He said: "I am not doing websites that much anymore but instead I am learning about Bitcoin." I immediately thought: "Oh damn, you fell for that scam as well?" And he started explaining to me not about the price going up or down and how you can get rich quickly, but how Bitcoin is really helping in the unbanked regions of the world.

"That got me curious, right? So I started reading everything I could find about Bitcoin. And I mean everything, including Bitcoin whitepaper, forums, YouTube videos, whatever. Got obsessed with understanding how it all worked."

Sunil nodded. "So when did you start actual mining?"

"I'm getting there," Dusan laughed. "So I read about mining and thought, why not try it? I had this gaming PC with a decent graphics card. Figured I could make some easy money on the side."

He shook his head, chuckling at the memory. "Man, was I wrong. First of all, I had no clue what I was doing. Downloaded some mining software and my computer fan started screaming like it was about to take off. The room got hotter than I could bear. And after like 24 hours of mining, I'd made about 50 cents. Meanwhile, my electricity bill was going to be way higher than that."

"So what happened?" Sunil asked, waving at the waiter for more beers.

Dusan scratched his beard. "Well... I figured out real quick that my simple laptop wasn't going to make me rich. That boat already sailed, you know? But I was kind of hooked by then. Got the mining bug. So I started obsessing over the serious mining gear, the ASIC equipment."

"You mean those noisy box things from today? At that booth?"

"Yeah those. ASIC. The point is, they're like special computers that do exactly ONE thing, that is Bitcoin mining. Not like graphics cards that can do gaming and stuff too."

The waiter showed up with two more beers and Dusan pointed at some desserts other people were eating. "Please get me one of those," he said, then turned back to Sunil. "You have to try the strudel here, it's insane."

Sunil picked at a loose thread on his sleeve. "So graphics cards, those are the GPU things gamers are always whining about being expensive?"

"Exactly!" Dusan took a big gulp of fresh beer. "So GPUs were what everyone used back in the day. Guys would have these Frankenstein rigs with like 6 graphics cards all duck taped together or whatever. Super bulgy setups." He laughed, wiping foam from his lip. "Some coins still use GPUs, but Bitcoin? Nah, that ship sailed years ago. All ASICs now."

"How come?"

Their desserts arrived and Dusan immediately took a big bite of his strudel. "Mmmpf," he started talking before swallowing, then caught himself. "Sorry. Anyway, it's just way more efficient. Like, a GPU can do lots of stuff, like games, video editing, mining different coins. But an ASIC does ONE thing and it does it like... a thousand times better."

"But they're really expensive. Actually, ridiculously expensive. And totally useless for anything else. Like, if Bitcoin changed how it works tomorrow or crashed to zero, you'd have a really expensive doorstop."

Sunil drank some beer, thinking. "So... what'd you end up doing?"

"Saved up for months. Found this guy online selling a used Antminer... S9 I think? Guy was bailing after prices tanked. So I got it pretty cheap. Set it up in my apartment..." Dusan rolled his eyes dramatically. "BIG mistake."

"Why?"

"These things are unbelievably loud man. Like having a vacuum cleaner running 24/7. And hot? Jeez. Turned my place into a sauna. All of my visitors were irritated." He snorted into his beer. Sunil laughed.

"But whatever. I eventually found this cheap warehouse space on the edge of town. Started with just my one little miner, then slowly added more whenever I had extra cash. Put everything back into it. Got obsessed with the efficiency stuff."

"And that's when you decided to go full throttle?"

"Kind of. The mining thing was actually making decent money. Enough that I could focus on it full-time. Then I started helping other miners set up their operations, doing consulting and stuff..." he vaguely waved his fork around, dropping a piece of strudel on the table, "...and now I'm here, getting you drunk and talking about hash functions."

Sunil laughed. "OK so how does the whole thing actually work? Like, what's the software side? You plug these loud boxes in and then what?"

Dusan grabbed a napkin and dug in his pocket. "Got a pen?" A nearby diner overheard and offered one. "Thanks man." He started scribbling on the napkin.

"So the hardware is these ASIC things, right? But you need software to run the show." He drew some boxes and lines, accidentally tearing the thin napkin. "OK so mining software does a bunch of stuff. It connects to the Bitcoin network so you can grab all the transactions that need verifying."

He kept drawing, now with beer stains adding to his masterpiece. "It also controls your miners, makes sure they're not overheating or whatever. And it shows you how well you're doing. That's your hash rate and stuff."

"Hash rate?"

"Yeah so remember how miners are solving puzzles? Hash rate is basically how many guesses your machine can make each second when trying to solve the mining puzzle."

He scribbled some numbers on the beer-soaked napkin. "Modern miners are measured in terahashes per second. That's TRILLIONS of attempts per second. My first miner did like... 14 terahashes? I thought that was hot back then. New ones do way over 200 now."

"Wait," Sunil squinted, trying to visualize it. "Trillions of attempts every SECOND? And it STILL takes 10 minutes to mine a block?"

"Yup. And that's with thousands and thousands of miners all hammering away. The difficulty thing adjusts to keep it at 10 minutes, no matter how much computing powcr is throwing guesses at it."

Sunil picked up his beer, put it down without drinking. "OK but what exactly IS a hash? You keep saying that word."

"Right, right," Dusan said, grabbing another napkin. "So a hash is like... OK, imagine you have this magic meat grinder. You put in any amount of stuff, it could be a single word or the entire text of the

Bible. The grinder always spits out a string of letters and numbers that's the same length. That's your hash."

He scribbled an example, beer dripping from his sleeve onto the napkin. "Crap. Anyway, like if I put 'hello' into the hash function, I get back this long string of gibberish. But the cool part is that if I change even ONE letter, like capitalizing the H in 'Hello', I get a completely different output. Like, totally different."

"And this matters because...?"

"Because that's how the whole blockchain security thing works!" Dusan said, getting animated and almost knocking over his beer. "Each block has the hash of the block before it. So if some person tries to go back and change even a tiny thing in an old block, that block's hash changes. And then the next block's reference doesn't match, and the whole chain breaks from that point forward."

He took a long swig of beer, belched quietly. "Excuse me. So when miners are fighting to add the next block, they're hunting for a special hash. They take all the transactions, add a random number called a nonce, and keep trying different nonces until they get a hash that starts with a certain number of zeros."

"And this happens trillions of times a second?"

"Exactly! It's a giant lottery, and the more hash power you've got, the more lottery tickets you're buying every second."

Their conversation paused as a waiter came by. Dusan ordered another round, his words slightly slurring now.

"So here's what I don't get," Sunil said, pushing away his empty plate. "If it's getting harder and harder, and you need these expensive machines eating electricity like crazy... how do you not go broke?"

"NOW we're getting to the good stuff!" Dusan leaned forward, accidentally dipping his sleeve in a smear of sauce. "Dammit. Whatever. So for miners, electricity is the killer. The machines are expensive up front, sure, but power bills just keep coming and coming."

He tried to draw some calculations, but gave up after messing up twice. "Miners obsess over this efficiency ratio thing, about how much power it takes to do a terahash. First ASICs were super wasteful. New ones are like... 8 times better. Maybe more."

"That's... good?" Sunil guessed.

"Of course it's good! Means I can mine the same amount and pay way less for power. Or mine 8 times more with the same electric bill."

"So as long as they keep making better machines, mining stays profitable?"

"That's part of it," Dusan said, excitedly. "But the location is HUGE. Electricity costs are all over the place. In Prague, it might be 15-20 cents per kilowatt hour. In Iceland or Ethiopia? Maybe 3-4 cents. That's why miners keep moving operations to weird places."

"Like that woman today... from the panel. Kazakhstan hydro dam lady."

"EXACTLY!" Dusan slapped the table, making the dishes jump. "Sorry. But yeah, miners are like electricity bloodhounds. We sniff out excess power nobody wants. Hydro dams during spring when there's too much water, gas that would just be burned off at oil wells, solar farms in the desert with no transmission lines... we soak it all up."

Dusan stared into his beer, suddenly philosophical. "It's actually kind of beautiful, you know? Bitcoin mining creates this global market for energy. Some random power plant in Mongolia can sell to the Bitcoin network if nobody around wants it."

"Never thought about it like that."

"Nobody does, man! They just read some headline about 'Bitcoin uses as much power as Denmark' or whatever and freak out. But it's way more nuanced."

Sunil nodded, trying to process everything through his beer haze. "So back to your story. You built up this mining operation, but it keeps getting harder. Are you still making money?"

"It's definitely rougher now," Dusan admitted, his shoulders slumping a bit. "Had to adapt. I'm constantly hunting for cheaper electricity. Moved my whole operation twice in three years. And I'm always upgrading to the newest gear whenever I can afford it."

"Sounds a bit stressful."

"Can be," Dusan shrugged. "But also kind of fun? It's like this constant puzzle. And I believe in Bitcoin long-term, so even when profits are dry, I feel like I'm supporting something important."

The restaurant had emptied out a lot. Through the windows, Sunil could see people wandering the streets, starting their night out.

"One last thing," Sunil said, finishing his beer. "Think I could do it? Mining I mean. Or is it too late?"

Dusan scratched his chin, looking thoughtful. "Real talk? Small mining is not viable now. You need cash up front, have to know your technical stuff, and cheap power is a must. For most normal people, it's probably easier to just buy some Bitcoin."

Sunil's face fell a bit, and Dusan quickly added, "But there are still ways in! Could start small, you know? Learn the ropes. I could help you figure something out."

Sunil perked up. "I'd be into that. Got time off from the ship anyway. And this whole thing is... pretty interesting."

"It is," Dusan nodded too enthusiastically. "And hey, even if mining's not your thing, there's tons of other Bitcoin stuff. Tomorrow at the conference we can check out some different angles."

"Deal." They clinked glasses sloppily.

The waiter brought their bill, and Dusan fumbled with his phone. "Want to see something cool? I can actually check my miners right now." He showed Sunil a screen with graphs and numbers, squinting to focus on it. "See this? Current hash rate. And this? Today's mining rewards."

Sunil leaned over. "Pretty sweet setup. You just control everything from your phone?"

"Most of it, yeah. Not like the old days. Now it's all high-tech and stuff. Got sensors for temperature, humidity, power usage... software adjusts everything automatically."

They paid and stumbled out into the cool night air, which felt good after the warm restaurant. Prague looked amazing at night, all lit up with the castle glowing across the river.

"Thanks for dinner," Sunil said as they wobbled back toward their hotel. "And for explaining all the mining stuff. I think I finally get why you're so obsessed."

"No problem," Dusan replied, narrowly avoiding a street sign. "Nice having someone actually interested in how it works. Most people just want to know how to get rich quick."

"I mean, that too," Sunil laughed. "But I really want to understand what I'm getting into first."

"Smart," Dusan said, clumsily patting Sunil's shoulder. "That's the way to do it. Tomorrow we'll get into the economic side. About how Bitcoin actually gets its value. That's when it really clicks."

"Looking forward to it," Sunil said. And seriously enough, he actually meant it.

CHAPTER 5
SETTING UP YOUR OWN BITCOIN MINING OPERATION

Sunil woke up with a mild headache and the taste of stale beer in his mouth. He fumbled for his phone on the nightstand. 8:47 AM. Shit. They were supposed to meet in the hotel lobby at 9 to head back to the conference.

He stumbled to the bathroom, splashed cold water on his face, and tried to piece together everything Dusan had told him last night about mining. His memories were a bit fuzzy around the edges, but he remembered being fascinated by the whole concept.

When he made it down to the lobby at 9:12, Dusan was slumped in an armchair, sunglasses on, nursing what looked like the world's largest coffee.

"Morning, sunshine," Dusan mumbled. "You look like I feel."

"Sorry I'm late," Sunil said, wincing at the sound of his own voice. "Too much beer last night."

"Czech beer is no joke," Dusan agreed, pushing himself up with effort. "But totally worth it. Come on, let's grab coffee and food at the conference. Day two is usually better anyway. Less crowded, more actual information."

The morning air was crisp and cool, helping clear Sunil's head as they walked. The streets of Prague were already bustling with tourists and locals. When they reached the conference centre, it was indeed noticeably less crowded than the day before.

"Thank god," Dusan said as they grabbed coffees and pastries from a stand near the entrance. "Let's find somewhere to sit and fuel up before we dive in."

They found a quiet corner with a small table away from the main floor. Sunil took a long sip of his coffee and immediately felt more human.

"So," he said after a moment, "last night you mentioned maybe helping me figure out if mining could work for me. Were you just drunk talking or did you mean it?"

Dusan pushed his sunglasses up onto his head and grinned. "I meant it. But I was definitely drunk. Still got the headache to prove it." He took a bite of pastry. "You serious about looking into it?"

"Yeah, actually. I've got some savings sitting around, and I'm not due back on a ship for at least three months. Might be a cool project."

"Alright then," Dusan said, perking up a bit. "Day two of BTC Prague is perfect for this. The first day is the big picture stuff. Today's when they get into the nuts and bolts."

He pulled out his phone and checked the schedule. "Perfect. There's a whole track on mining setup for beginners at 10:30. But let me give you a quick overview first, since we've got time."

Dusan grabbed a napkin out of habit, then laughed. "No, I'm not drawing on another napkin. Just cleaning my hands, so I don't smudge my phone."

Instead, he pulled out his phone and opened his notes app. "OK, so if you're serious about setting up a mining operation, there are six main things to consider."

He typed as he talked: "Hardware, location, setup, pool vs solo, software config, and profitability calculations."

"First up, hardware," he continued. "You saw those ASIC miners yesterday. To do this right, you need to think about a few key factors."

He counted on his fingers. "One, hash rate. That's how many calculations per second the machine can do. The computing power of the machines is similar to horse power in cars. Higher is better but costs more. Two, efficiency. How much electricity it uses to generate this hash rate. Three, reliability. Some models break down constantly, others run forever. This is often the case due to mal-manufacturing."

"And four," he added, "is machine price, obviously. Newest models can cost thousands, but you can find used ones for much less. Just gotta be careful not to buy some piece of junk."

Sunil nodded, making mental notes. "What about cooling? You mentioned they get super-hot."

"Huge issue," Dusan agreed. "These things are basically space heaters that make money. If they overheat, they perform worse or even shut down. So whatever space you set up in needs serious cooling. Notc that there are three different ways to cool your machine: Air, water, or oil."

He checked his watch. "Which brings us to location. This is the thing most newbies screw up. They buy expensive gear but put it in a terrible location."

"What makes a location terrible?" Sunil asked.

"Three things kill mining profitability: high electricity costs, poor internet connection, and bad cooling options."

Dusan finished his coffee. "Electricity is the big one, contributing around 80% of the operational costs. Mining rigs run 24/7, so your power bill gets massive. In some places, the cost of electricity is more than the Bitcoin you mine."

"Like where?"

"Germany, Denmark, parts of the US. Places with electricity over 10 cents per kilowatt hour make mining tough. That's why big operations are in places like Kazakhstan, Iceland, Ethiopia, Paraguay, parts of China, Texas... anywhere with cheap power."

Sunil frowned. "I'm not moving to Kazakhstan."

"You don't have to," Dusan laughed. "For a small operation, you just need to be aware of your local electricity rates. Maybe look into solar if you've got the space and money. Some miners even make deals with local power companies for off peak rates."

"Actually," Dusan continued, pulling up a website on his phone, "let me show you something about electricity costs. Ethiopia's perfect for mining. Nearly hundred percent renewable electricity, mostly hydropower. They offer power purchase agreements at 3.14 cents per kilowatt hour."

"That's cheap?"

"Incredibly cheap. But there's more to it," Dusan scrolled through some figures. "You need a legal framework too. Ethiopia actually ratified laws for 'data mining' and 'high performance computing' that specifically allow Bitcoin mining. Very important for customs and operations."

"What about other places?"

"Finland's interesting," Dusan said. "Their futures contracts can get you electricity at twenty five to thirty five euros per megawatt hour if you sell the heat back to district heating systems. Mining rigs generate loads of heat, so why waste it?"

They got up to throw away their trash, and Dusan continued as they walked toward the presentation halls.

"The internet is the second factor. You don't need super-fast speeds, but you need reliability. If your connection drops for hours, you lose mining time, which means lost money."

"And then cooling," he said, "which we already touched on. These machines run hot and noisy. You need good airflow, maybe extra fans, and a space where the noise won't drive you crazy or drive away the neighbours."

"Speaking of calculations," Sunil said as they walked, "how do you actually work out if mining is profitable? You mentioned calculators earlier."

"Ah, that's where hash price comes in," Dusan said, his eyes lighting up. "It's basically the revenue mining machines earn per unit of computational power. We measure it in terahashes per second, or TH/s."

Sunil frowned. "That sounds complicated."

"Not really," Dusan said, pulling up another website. "Let me show you with today's numbers. Right now, Bitcoin's at what... ninety nine thousand dollars."

"Bloody hell, that's high," Sunil muttered.

"Right? So here's how it works," Dusan continued. "Miners get rewards two ways. First, they earn Bitcoin for each block they mine. Currently, that's 3.125 bitcoin per block."

"How often do they mine blocks?"

"About every ten minutes on average. So that's roughly 144 blocks per day." Dusan did some quick maths. "That means around 450 bitcoins are generated daily across the entire network."

"But that gets split between all miners worldwide?"

"Exactly. Plus, there's transaction fees on top of that," Dusan said, navigating to mempool.space on his phone. "See this latest block? Block 895772. It earned 0.019 bitcoin just in transaction fees, on top of the standard 3.125 reward."

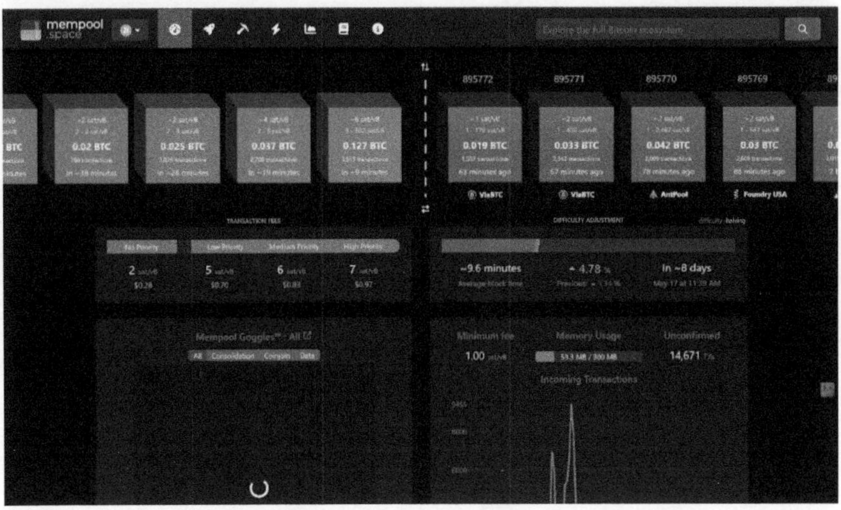

Sunil leaned in to look at the screen. "So miners compete for both the new Bitcoin and the fees?"

"Right. Some days the fees are huge, other days not so much," Dusan explained, switching to blockchain.com. "Here, let me show you how to check. Go to Explorer, then Charts, then Mining Information. Look at total transaction fees."

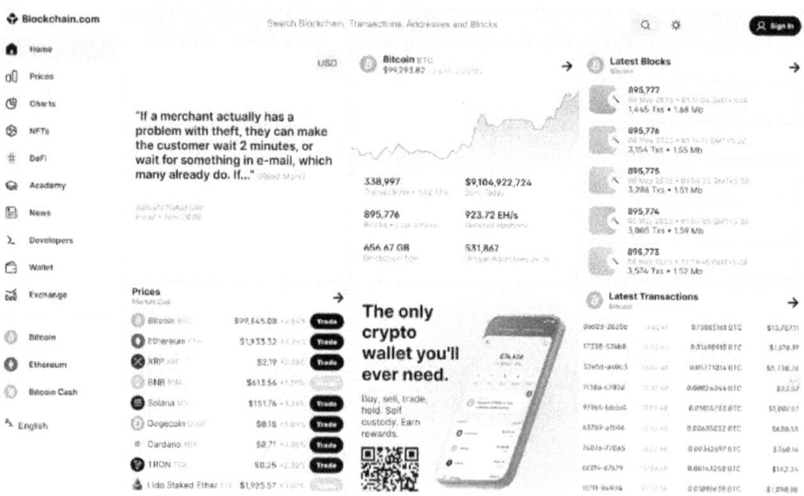

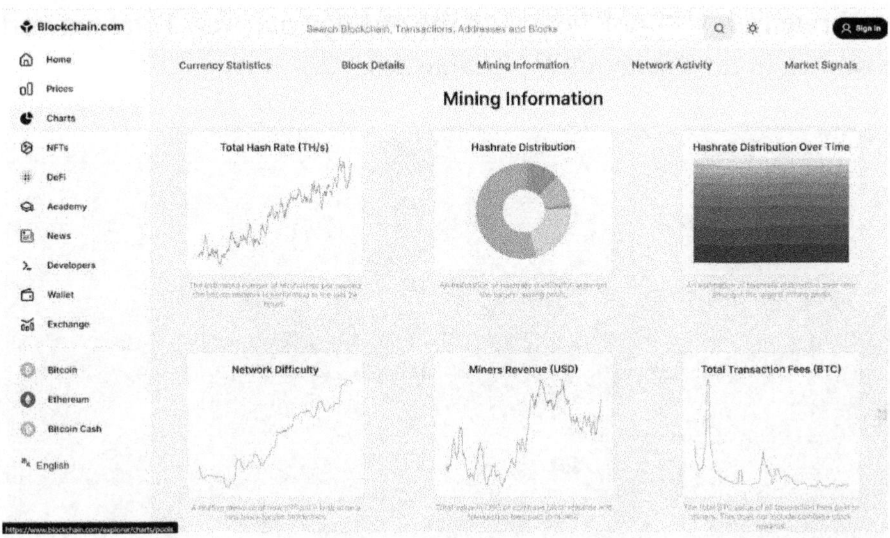

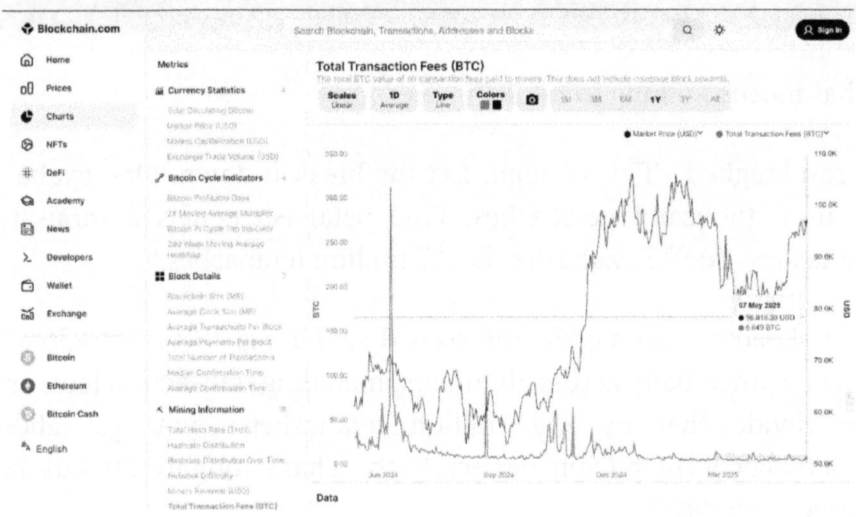

He hovered his finger over the chart. "Yesterday, May 7th, total transaction fees for the whole day were about 6.649 bitcoin. That's for all 144 blocks combined."

"How do you know what your share would be?"

"That's where global hashrate comes in," Dusan said, pulling up Hashrate Index. "Look here with the one day interval. Total network power right now is about 917 exahashes."

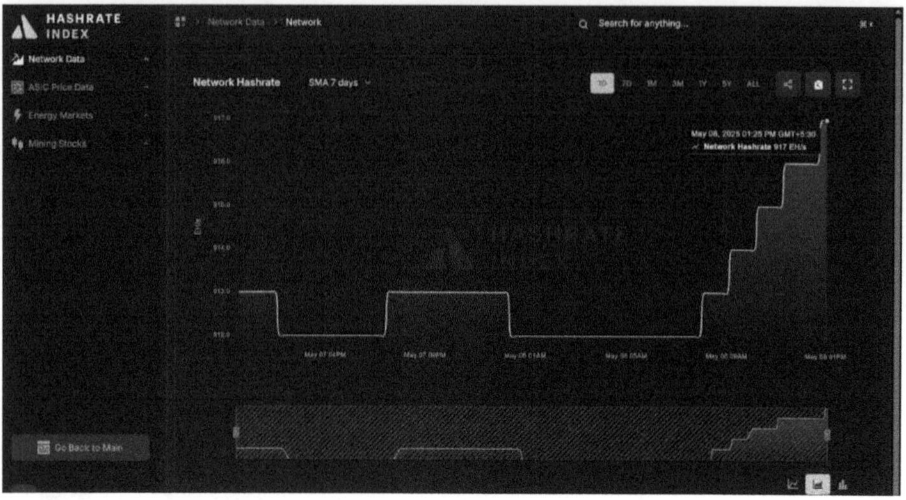

"That means nothing to me."

Dusan laughed. "Fair enough. Let me break it down. One exahash equals a thousand petahashes. One petahash equals a thousand terahashes. So 917 exahashes is 917 million terahashes."

He grabbed a fresh napkin and started scribbling. "If there's 456.649 bitcoin earned daily across all miners, including transaction fees, and you divide that by 917 million terahashes... you get about 0.0000004979814 bitcoin per terahash. That's roughly 50 sats per terahash per day."

"Sats?"

"Satoshis. Smallest unit of Bitcoin. Hundred million sats in one bitcoin." Dusan finished his calculation. "At today's prices, multiply that by 99,000 dollars, and you get about 4.9 cents per terahash per day."

Sunil studied the napkin. "So if I had that 120 terahash machine we saw earlier..."

"You'd make about 5.88 dollars per day in revenue," Dusan finished. "Before electricity costs, of course."

They reached the hall where the mining setup presentation would be held. It was already filling up with people clutching coffees and laptops.

"Looks popular," Sunil noted.

"Everyone wants to be a miner until they realize how much work it is," Dusan said with a smirk. "Let's grab seats near the front."

As they settled in, a woman in a Bitcoin t-shirt was setting up her presentation. Dusan nodded toward her.

"Maria. She runs a medium sized mining operation in Paraguay. Really knows her stuff."

The presentation began right on time. The slides showed detailed pictures of mining setups ranging from small home operations to massive warehouses.

"The key to successful mining," Maria began in slightly accented English, "is proper setup from day one. Many beginners make costly mistakes that could be avoided with proper planning."

She clicked to a slide showing a step by step setup process. "First, you need a dedicated space. Even a small mining rig generates heat and noise. A spare room, garage, or basement works for beginners."

The next slide showed electrical requirements. "Most ASICs require 220 volt connections, similar to large appliances like dryers. You may need an electrician to install proper outlets and ensure your wiring can handle the load."

Dusan leaned over to Sunil. "That's super important. Regular outlets can't handle these machines. People try to use adapters and end up with electrical fires."

Maria continued, displaying images of various cooling setups. "Airflow is critical. Hot air must be exhausted and cool air brought in. For home setups, this could be as simple as window fans, but ideally you want dedicated intake and exhaust systems."

She switched to a slide showing a rack of miners with elaborate ducting. "In larger operations, we use industrial cooling systems. But for beginners, good fans and proper spacing between machines is sufficient."

Sunil scribbled notes on his phone as she spoke, occasionally nudging Dusan with questions.

The presentation moved on to network configuration, with diagrams of routers and switches connected to mining rigs.

"A stable internet connection is essential," Maria emphasized. "While bandwidth requirements are minimal, reliability is crucial. Consider redundant connections if possible."

She clicked to a new section: "Solo Mining vs. Pool Mining."

"For most miners today, especially beginners, pool mining is the only realistic option," she explained. "In a mining pool, you combine your hash power with other miners and share the rewards proportionally."

A graph appeared showing mining rewards over time for solo versus pool mining.

"Solo mining means attempting to mine blocks alone. With current network difficulty, a small miner might go years without finding a block. Pools provide smaller but regular pay-outs."

Dusan nodded along. "She's right. Solo mining is basically playing the lottery. Pools give you steady income based on your contribution. It's less exciting but much more practical."

Maria moved on to a slide listing popular mining pools. "When choosing a pool, consider fees, pay-out methods, server locations, and reputation. Most charge between 1 to 3 percent of your earnings."

The final section of her presentation covered software configuration. Screenshots of mining software interfaces filled the screen.

"Once your hardware is set up, you'll need to configure your mining software. Most ASIC miners come with factory software, but you may want to install third party firmware for better control and performance."

She demonstrated adjusting settings for overclocking, fan speeds, and power limits. "Finding the right balance between performance and efficiency requires experimentation. Too aggressive, and you risk hardware failure. Too conservative, and you leave money on the table."

As the presentation wrapped up, Maria expanded on some practical costs. "Now, let's talk real numbers. Setting up in a place like Ethiopia, your base PPA might be 3.14 cents. But add 15 percent VAT, that's 0.471 cents. Add regulatory fees of 0.5 percent, another 0.0157 cents. Your actual cost is about 3.63 cents per kilowatt hour."

She clicked to another slide. "Infrastructure costs matter too. A one megawatt air cooled container costs around 50,000 dollars. If you amortize that over two years of operation, it adds roughly 0.29 cents per kilowatt hour to your costs."

"Don't forget operations and maintenance," she continued. "Professional management companies charge 0.3 to 0.4 cents per kilowatt hour. All in, you're looking at 4.2 to 4.5 cents before considering land lease."

Someone from the audience asked about hosting partners versus self-operation.

"Good question," Maria replied. "For operations under 10 megawatts, hosting partners usually make more sense. They charge about 5 to 5.5 cents per kilowatt hour for a one megawatt capacity. No capital expenditure, no operational headaches. They handle everything."

As people filed out after the presentation, Dusan and Sunil stayed seated, continuing their conversation.

"So what did you think?" Dusan asked. "Still interested, or did she scare you off?"

Sunil laughed. "Actually, I'm more interested now. It sounds complicated, but not impossible. Kind of like maintaining engines on a ship. Lots of moving parts to monitor, but follow the procedures and you're fine."

"That's a good way to look at it," Dusan agreed. "So, do you want to check out some hardware? There's an exhibition area where you can see different mining rigs up close."

They made their way to the exhibition floor, which was less crowded than the day before. Various vendors had set up booths displaying mining equipment, cooling systems, and software solutions.

At one booth, a sales rep was demonstrating the latest Antminer model. "This beauty does 270 terahashes per second at just 3645 watts," he boasted. "S21 XP, Most efficient on the market right now."

Dusan examined it with a critical eye. "What's the price point?"

"Just 5,700 euro," the rep said smoothly. "But they're backordered two months."

"See what I mean about costs?" Dusan muttered to Sunil as they moved on. "But there are other options."

They stopped at a booth selling refurbished miners. The units looked a bit worn but were priced at less than half of the new models.

"Something like this might be a good starter unit," Dusan suggested. "Not the latest and greatest, but still profitable if your electricity costs are reasonable."

Sunil checked the specs: 120 TH/s, 2760 watts. "How do I know if that's good enough?"

"Remember the hashprice calculation I showed you?" Dusan pulled out his phone again. "Let's work it through properly. If the current hashprice is about 4.9 cents per terahash per day, and this machine does 120 terahashes..."

He typed quickly. "That's 5.88 dollars revenue per day. The machine uses 2760 watts, which is 2.76 kilowatts. Running 24 hours, that's 66.24 kilowatt hours per day."

"At European average of 15 cents per kilowatt hour," he continued calculating, "that's 9.94 dollars in electricity costs. So you'd actually lose money."

Sunil's face fell. "That's depressing."

"But," Dusan said, "at Ethiopian rates of 5 cents all in with hosting, it's only 3.31 dollars in costs. Profit of 2.57 dollars per day. Not amazing, but it adds up."

"That's why location matters so much," Sunil said, as he began to understand.

"Exactly. The same machine can be highly profitable or a money pit, depending entirely on your electricity costs."

They continued browsing the exhibition, stopping to examine cooling systems, power management tools, and monitoring software.

At a small booth in the corner, a guy was demonstrating immersion cooling, where the miners were completely submerged in a non-conductive fluid.

"This is the future of mining cooling," he insisted. "Extends hardware life, reduces noise, and improves efficiency by up to 20 percent."

Dusan looked genuinely impressed. "He's not wrong. Immersion is amazing, but the setup cost is high for beginners, and you can't place oil systems everywhere."

As they explored, Dusan shared more insights about procurement. "One thing I learnt the hard way - never buy miners without checking if the manufacturer has a repair centre in your hosting country."

"Why's that?"

"Warranty repairs. If something breaks and there's no local support, you have to ship the miner to the nearest service centre. Costs a fortune and takes weeks. Always check with OEMs like Bitmain or MicroBT about their service network."

"What about buying the actual machines?" Sunil asked as they passed another vendor booth.

"For small orders under a hundred units, go with reputable resellers. LeedMiner, Letine Mining, JSBIT, BitMars, MinerSource. They're established and reliable." Dusan paused at a display of various ASIC models. "For bigger orders over 500 units, deal directly with manufacturers."

"Any other tips?"

"Several," Dusan said, counting on his fingers. "First, avoid first batch releases. They always have issues. Hashboards overheat, heat sinks come loose. Plus they're more expensive. Wait for the second or third batch."

"Second, stick with Hong Kong or China manufactured units when possible. Some batches from Malaysia or Thailand have had quality issues."

"Third, always verify warranty periods. Standard is twelve months from manufacture date, but resellers sometimes sell older stock. You can check the remaining warranty by entering serial numbers on the manufacturer's website."

"And finally," he continued, "factor in shipping and customs. Some places allow DDP - delivery duty paid. Others like Ethiopia only do DDU - delivery duty unpaid. The local hosting company handles customs clearance, usually about 3 percent."

"What's the difference between those two?" Sunil asked, looking confused.

"Good question," Dusan smiled. "With DDP, it's like ordering something online to your house. The freight forwarder or courier company takes care of everything, including customs. The package gets delivered straight to your door, all duties and taxes already paid. Super convenient."

"And DDU?"

"DDU means you have to handle the customs bit yourself. The package arrives at your local customs office, but then you or your hosting company needs to go there, fill out paperwork, pay the duties and taxes, and collect it. More hassle, but sometimes it works out cheaper if you have good local connections."

By lunchtime, they'd explored most of the exhibition floor. They grabbed sandwiches from a café inside the venue and found a table near a window overlooking the city.

"So," Dusan said between bites, "after seeing all that, what are you thinking? Still want to try mining?"

Sunil thought for a moment. "I think so, yeah. Maybe start small like you said. One decent unit to learn on."

"That's smart," Dusan nodded. "And hey, I've got some connections that might get you a decent deal on a used Whatsminer. Not as flashy as an Antminer, but solid machines."

"What about location though? I'm traveling most of the time."

Dusan considered this. "That's trickier. Mining rigs need regular monitoring. You could look into hosting services. They provide space, power, and maintenance for your machines for a monthly fee."

"That's a thing?"

"Absolutely. Lots of miners don't want the hassle of running their own facility. Hosting companies handle everything. You just own the hardware and collect the mining rewards, minus their fee."

"How do I choose a good hosting partner?" Sunil asked, making notes.

"Several factors," Dusan explained. "First, check their track record. Ask for uptime reports and client testimonials. A good host should show you their PPA agreement, even if they won't give you a copy."

"Second, verify their legal status. In Ethiopia, you can check with the Ethiopian Investment Commission. Make sure they have proper licenses and can legally import miners."

"Third, technical support. You want 24/7 availability and good relationships with manufacturer repair centres. Ask about typical turnaround times for repairs."

"And pricing?" Sunil prompted.

"Be wary of prices way below market rate. Might mean corners are being cut. As Maria said, expect 5 to 5.5 cents for one megawatt hosting. Some offer better rates with capital expenditure commitments."

"There's another consideration," Dusan added. "Some hosting companies can procure miners for you. Saves shipping hassles, but always get proper invoices and verify warranties."

Sunil pulled out his phone and made detailed notes. "Any hosting companies you recommend?"

"Several, actually. Some have direct PPAs with government utilities, others sublease from larger operations. Both can work, but direct PPA holders usually offer more stability. I can make introductions."

They finished their lunch, and Dusan checked the schedule again. "There's a workshop on setting up mining software at 2. Wanna check it out?"

"Definitely," Sunil said. "If I'm gonna do this, I want to understand every part of it."

The software workshop was hands on, with participants following along on laptops. The instructor walked them through configuring Braiins OS, a popular mining firmware.

"First, you'll need to find your miner's IP address on your network," he explained. "Then access the web interface to install the new firmware."

Dusan and Sunil shared a laptop, with Dusan guiding through the configuration process. The interface was complex but logical, with settings for power limits, fan control, and pool configuration.

"See this section here?" Dusan pointed. "This is where you enter your mining pool information. The URL, your wallet address, and sometimes a worker name to identify this specific machine."

Sunil nodded, absorbing the information. "And these temperature settings?"

"Critical," Dusan emphasized. "Set your target chip temperature and fan speed rules. If it gets too hot, you want it to throttle back automatically to prevent damage."

The instructor demonstrated advanced features. "For maximum efficiency, you'll want to experiment with overclocking and undervolting. Every machine has a sweet spot where it delivers optimal hash rate per watt."

"But be careful," he warned. "Push too hard and you'll damage the hardware. Start conservative and gradually increase."

By the end of the workshop, they had configured a virtual mining setup from start to finish. The instructor provided downloadable guides for various mining models to reference later.

As the conference day wound down, they found themselves back at the terrace overlooking the river, the same spot they'd talked the day before. The afternoon sun cast a golden glow over Prague's skyline.

"So," Dusan said, leaning on the railing, "after two days of Bitcoin immersion, what's your verdict? Still think I'm crazy for giving up sailing for this?"

Sunil laughed. "Maybe a little crazy, but I get it now. It's like... building and maintaining your own money generating machine. There's something satisfying about that."

"Exactly!" Dusan exclaimed. "It's not just about the profit, though that's nice. It's about being part of this new financial system, running the infrastructure that makes it work. Contributing actively by providing value by securing the network is very satisfying work."

"So what's next?" Sunil asked. "The conference is ending. You heading back to your mining operation?"

"Yeah, back to the daily grind tomorrow. Got to check on some new machines we're bringing online. But I've got some things to wrap up here first." Dusan turned to face him. "What about you?"

Sunil looked out over the city, thinking. "I think I'm gonna do it. Start small like you suggested. Maybe one good ASIC to learn on, see if I can make it work."

"That's the spirit. Start with one machine, learn the ropes, then scale up if it makes sense." Dusan grinned. "And hey, I'm happy to help. Mining's more fun when you're not figuring it all out alone."

"I appreciate that," Sunil said sincerely. "This whole Bitcoin thing was just a vague concept to me a few days ago. Now I'm calculating hashprices and planning to buy mining equipment. Funny how things turn out."

"Life's full of surprises," Dusan agreed. "Two years ago I was sailing on cruisers across the Mediterranean. Now I'm running servers that secure a global financial network. Never would have predicted that."

"Speaking of which," Sunil said, "any final advice for a complete newcomer?"

Dusan thought for a moment. "Yeah. Don't rush into it. Take time to understand the numbers. Visit a hosting facility if you can. Join online mining communities. And always, always do your due diligence on hosting partners and equipment sellers."

"And remember," he added, "mining isn't passive income. It's a business. Treat it seriously, stay informed about network changes, and be ready to adapt. The most successful miners are those who never stop learning."

As the sun began to set, casting long shadows across the ancient city, the two friends continued talking about mining specifics, hardware recommendations, and next steps. For Sunil, it was the beginning of a new adventure. For Dusan, it was a chance to share his passion with someone who finally understood it.

The Bitcoin conference had opened a door, and Sunil was ready to step through it, one mining rig at a time.

CHAPTER 6

CHOOSING AND EVALUATING BITCOIN MINING HOSTING SERVICES

"Meet me at Charles Bridge at four," Dusan had texted. "Got something to show you."

Sunil checked his watch. 3:52 PM. He'd spent the morning after the conference browsing mining equipment online, his head swimming with specs and prices. The conference was over, but Dusan had offered to stick around an extra day to show him around Prague.

The bridge was packed with tourists taking selfies. Street performers and vendors lined the edges, creating a busy atmosphere. Sunil leaned against the stone railing, watching boats cruise below on the Vltava River.

"There you are!" Dusan's voice came from behind. "Sorry I'm late. I was on a call with my facility manager. Some cooling issues."

"No problem," Sunil said, turning around. "Nice spot. Totally different vibe from the conference."

"Right? Figured we needed a break from all that indoor tech talk." Dusan grinned. "Besides, you can't visit Prague without seeing Charles Bridge."

They started walking slowly, dodging the occasional selfie stick.

"So," Dusan continued, "I've been thinking about your situation. You want to mine, but you're on ships half the year. Not exactly ideal for machines that need daily attention."

"Yeah, been wondering about that," Sunil admitted. "Hard to fix a mining rig from the middle of the ocean."

"Exactly. Which is why hosting facilities might be perfect for you."

They paused at a lookout point, taking in the view of Prague's red rooftops.

"Hosting facilities?" Sunil asked. "You mentioned those briefly, right? Places that house your mining equipment?"

"Yep. Think of them like hotels for your miners," Dusan explained. "You buy the hardware, they provide space, power, internet, cooling, and maintenance. You pay a monthly fee, and they keep your machines running while you collect the Bitcoin."

A street musician started playing nearby, the melody floating over the bridge noise.

"Sounds convenient," Sunil nodded. "But expensive, yeah?"

"Can be," Dusan acknowledged. "But for someone who can't babysit equipment 24/7, it's worth it. And with the right facility, the math works in your favour."

They reached the end of the bridge and found a small cafe with outdoor seating.

"Let's grab a coffee," Dusan suggested. "I'll walk you through how these places work."

Once settled with their drinks, Dusan pulled out his tablet. "So, hosting facilities range from small converted warehouses to massive data centres built just for mining."

He showed Sunil photos of several facilities: rows of mining rigs, cooling systems, and technicians working.

"Damn," Sunil muttered, looking at a particularly large operation. "That looks like a sci-fi movie. How many miners are there?"

"That's Galaxy Digital in Texas. About 80,000 ASICs running at once. One of the biggest in the world," Dusan said. "But there are plenty of smaller ones better for beginners."

Sunil sipped his coffee. "What should I look for in a hosting facility?"

Dusan counted on his fingers. "Five main things: cost, uptime, cooling, reputation of the operator, and location."

"Cost is obvious," he continued. "Most facilities charge per kilowatt hour, usually a fixed rate above the base electricity cost. So if electricity is 5 cents per kWh, they might charge 8 cents. That 3 cent markup covers their overhead, staff, and profit."

"That doesn't sound terrible," Sunil said.

"It adds up when running 24/7, but good facilities keep it reasonable. Some charge a flat monthly fee instead. Others do profit sharing where they take a percentage of what you mine."

Dusan pulled up a comparison chart. "Here's a breakdown of different pricing models. For beginners, I usually recommend flat kWh pricing. It's the most transparent."

A waiter refilled their water, and Dusan waited before continuing.

"Next is uptime. This is HUGE. Every minute your machines are offline, you're losing money. Good facilities guarantee 97 percent uptime or better. Ask about backup power, redundant internet, and their track record during outages."

Sunil nodded. "Makes sense. What about cooling?"

"Critical," Dusan emphasized. "These machines run hot as hell, and heat kills ASICs over time. Cheap facilities try to get by with basic fans. The good ones have real cooling systems."

He showed different cooling setups. "You've got traditional air cooling with industrial systems, immersion cooling where machines sit in special fluid, and even some places using the heat for warming buildings or greenhouses."

"Which is best?"

"Depends. Hydro is most efficient but most expensive. Good air cooling works fine if done right. The key is what temperatures they maintain. Ask for temperature data. If they can't provide it, run away."

Sunil watched tourists walk by. "And location? Cheaper electricity is better?"

"That's the big one. The mining landscape is always changing based on energy costs and regulations. Right now, hot spots are parts of the US like Texas or Oklahoma, then Kazakhstan, Ethiopia, Paraguay, and some Nordic countries."

Dusan showed a world map with highlighted regions. "These areas have the magic combo: cheap power, cool climate, and good regulations."

"So I should just pick whatever's cheapest?" Sunil asked.

"Not necessarily," Dusan warned. "Consider political stability too. No point saving on electricity if the government might seize your equipment next year. Always consider the risk-reward ratio."

"Good point," Sunil conceded. "Who are the big players in hosting? Anyone you would recommend?"

Dusan took a long sip before answering. "There are established names: Compute North, Bitfarms, Marathon, Core Scientific, Hut 8. These are publicly traded companies with massive operations."

He switched screens on his tablet. "Then mid-sized players like Blockware Solutions, Compass Mining in North American Sector, AmityAge, Terahash, Hashlabs in Finland & Ethiopian Sector. More affordable but still professional."

"For beginners, smaller operations can be good. They're more flexible with better customer service. I know a good one in Iceland run by an old sailing buddy, actually. Super reliable guy."

A guitarist started playing nearby, adding pleasant background music.

"But how do I know who to trust?" Sunil asked. "Seems like I'd just be sending expensive equipment to strangers and hoping for the best."

"Valid worry," Dusan nodded. "Never go with a facility you can't verify. Check reviews, ask for client references, see if they're properly registered."

He scrolled through his contacts. "I can introduce you to some hosts I've worked with. No pressure to use them, but at least you'll have a starting point."

"That would be great," Sunil said. "So assuming I find a trustworthy place, how do the contracts work?"

"Contracts typically run 6 to 24 months. Longer commitments usually get better rates. You'll want to negotiate a few key points."

He listed them off: "Power limits and costs. Make sure there's a cap on what they can charge, even if local rates increase. Maintenance responsibilities, who pays if something breaks. Uptime guarantees and response times. And exit clauses, in case you need to pull your equipment."

"Sounds complicated," Sunil frowned.

"It can be," Dusan admitted. "But most hosts have standard contracts. You just need to read carefully and push back on anything unfavourable."

He pulled out a document and slid it across. "Here's a sample contract from a host I've used. I've highlighted the important areas."

Sunil scanned it, eyes widening. "Jeez, lots of fine print."

"Welcome to the business side of mining," Dusan laughed. "Not as exciting as watching Bitcoin roll in, but just as important."

They ordered another round of coffees.

"One thing people miss is negotiating leverage. If hosting facilities have empty racks, you've got leverage."

"How so?" Sunil asked.

"Setup fees are often flexible. Ask for a discount, especially with multiple machines. Try to get power costs closer to wholesale. Push for better maintenance terms, like 24/7 monitoring. And always ask for a trial period where you can remove your equipment without penalty if you're not satisfied."

The cafe has filled with tourists taking afternoon breaks. Sunil watched them, processing everything.

"Any red flags I should watch for?" he finally asked.

"Plenty," Dusan said. "Be suspicious of rates that seem too good. They're either lying or cutting corners. Avoid places that won't let you visit or won't share real time monitoring. And run from anyone asking for big upfront payments. That screams scam."

Sunil nodded, then asked, "You said visit in person. How can I do that if the best facilities are in Ethiopia?"

"Good question," Dusan said. "For international locations, look for virtual tours, live video calls from the facility, and client references. Or work with a broker who's vetted them personally."

Sunil pulled out his phone to make notes. "If I go with hosting, what's step one?"

"First, decide your budget and how many machines to start with," Dusan advised. "Even one ASIC is fine for learning. Then research hosting options in regions with cheap, stable power."

"Once you've narrowed down candidates, get quotes. Be specific about your equipment and needs. Compare proposals on all factors, not just price. Then negotiate better terms."

"And after picking a host?"

"Start small," Dusan emphasized. "Ship one machine, see how they handle it, monitor performance for a month. If it's good, then scale up."

Dusan pulled up an app on his phone. "Look, this is the dashboard for my hosted miners. I can see hash rates, temperatures, earnings, everything. I can even reboot machines remotely."

The interface showed real time data for several mining rigs, with charts and status indicators.

"That's pretty slick," Sunil admitted. "Definitely better than setting up something in my apartment and having it catch fire while I'm at sea."

Dusan laughed. "Exactly. For your lifestyle, hosting makes sense. You focus on what you're good at, let the pros handle daily operations."

They watched people pass by. The afternoon sun cast long shadows between buildings.

"Any other advice?" Sunil asked.

"Find a host who communicates well and is transparent. If they're dodgy with questions now, that won't improve once they have your hardware. You want someone who treats you like a partner, not just a customer."

"Makes sense," Sunil nodded. "What's your setup like?"

"I've got a hybrid approach. We at AmityAge have mining operations in Paraguay and Ethiopia. Spreads risk and takes advantage of different electricity prices."

"Smart," Sunil said. "Maybe I'll start with hosting, learn the ropes, then set up my own operation if I leave the ships."

"Could happen," Dusan smiled. "That's my story. Started with one hosted miner while sailing, got hooked, and here we are."

He checked his watch. "We should head out. I promised to show you Prague Castle before dinner."

As they paid and left, Sunil felt excited about his potential new venture. What started as a conference invitation was becoming a possible career change.

"Thanks for explaining all this," he said as they walked toward the castle. "I feel like I might actually be able to do this now."

"You definitely can," Dusan assured him. "And I'm just a text away if you need help. That's what the Bitcoin community is about. We help each other figure this stuff out."

The streets of Prague stretched before them, as did the possibilities of this mining adventure. Sunil had sought a break from life at sea and found something unexpected: a potential new path forward.

CHAPTER 7
UNDERSTANDING BITCOIN MINING ECONOMICS

Prague Castle was huge up close. Way bigger than it looked from the bridge. Sunil and Dusan walked through the place, checking out the weird Gothic church and the views from the walls.

"This place is freaking massive," Sunil said, staring up at the tall spires. "How old is it anyway?"

"Parts go back to like the 9th century," Dusan replied. "They kept adding on to it for hundreds of years. Kind of like Bitcoin mining, always changing and stuff."

Sunil snorted. "Do you seriously connect everything back to Bitcoin?"

"Pretty much," Dusan grinned. "Hey, there's a cafe in the garden with a killer view. Let's grab a seat. I want to talk about the money side of mining before we meet those local miners for dinner."

They found a table at the outdoor cafe with a view of the city below. The sun was getting low, making everything look orange and gold. A waiter took their order for coffee and some pastry things Dusan recommended.

"So," Dusan said once they got their stuff, "we've talked about the tech crap and hosting and whatever. But let's get to what everybody actually cares about: making money."

Sunil leaned in. "Yeah, I was wondering when we'd get to that part. How do miners actually get paid in bitcoin?"

"K, so remember how miners compete to solve those math puzzles?" Dusan stirred his coffee around and took a sip. "When a miner gets a block, they get two types of rewards. First, they get new bitcoin that's created with each block. Right now that's 3.125 bitcoin per block."

"They also get all the transaction fees from the people who had transactions in that block. Sometimes that's just a little extra, other days it can be almost as much as the block reward itself."

"So how often does a normal miner find a block?" Sunil asked.

Dusan laughed. "That's the thing. With your setup, mining by yourself? Probably never. It's so competitive now that a small miner might go like decades without finding anything."

"For real? Then what's the point?"

"That's why everybody joins mining pools," Dusan said. "Instead of trying to find whole blocks alone, you throw in your computing power with thousands of other miners. When anybody in the pool finds a block, everybody gets a cut based on how much they contributed."

Their pastries showed up, and Dusan took a big bite before going on.

"So instead of waiting forever for some huge payday that'll probably never happen, you get small payments every day or week, depending on how the pool pays out."

Sunil nodded. "Makes sense. How much could I expect to make from like one decent mining machine in a pool?"

"Depends on a bunch of stuff," Dusan said, pulling out his phone calculator. "The big one is mining difficulty."

"You talked about that before, but I don't really get it."

"Bitcoin is designed to make one block on average every 10 minutes, no matter how many miners are working," Dusan explained with his mouth half full. "To make that happen, there's this automatic adjustment more or less every two weeks."

He slurped some coffee. "If lots of new miners jump in and blocks are coming too fast, the difficulty goes up, making the puzzles harder. If miners quit and blocks are too slow, difficulty drops."

"So when more miners join, everybody makes less?" Sunil asked.

"You got it. Total bitcoin made each day stays the same, just split among more miners. That's why you have to keep an eye on the network hash rate."

"Hash rate is the total computing power on the network, right?"

"Exactly," Dusan nodded. "Over the years, bitcoin's total hash rate went from a few laptops to massive warehouse farms with special equipment. It's gone up like a trillion times since the beginning."

A bunch of loud tourists walked by their table taking pictures. Dusan waited for them to move on.

"Every time the network hash rate goes up, your slice of the pie gets smaller, assuming you don't add more machines."

Sunil frowned. "Doesn't sound great for new miners."

"It's harder now for sure," Dusan admitted. "But you can still make it work. Let me show you how to figure out what you might earn."

He grabbed a napkin and started writing. "Let's use the Bitmain T21 as an example. It does about 190 terahashes per second and uses around 3,610 watts of power."

He scribbled some numbers. "Remember our calculation from earlier? We worked out about 50 sats per terahash per day, which is 0.00000050 bitcoin. If bitcoin hits $100,000, that's about 5 cents per terahash."

Sunil watched as Dusan did the maths. "So for 190 terahashes, your daily revenue would be 190 times 5 cents, which gives us $9.50 per day."

"That sounds alright," Sunil said, leaning forward.

"Now for the costs," Dusan continued, tapping his pen. "At 3.61 kilowatts running all day, that's about 86.6 kilowatt hours per day. With hosting at 5 cents per kilowatt hour, that's $4.33 a day in power and hosting."

He finished the calculation. "So $9.50 in revenue minus $4.33 in operating costs gives you about $5.17 profit each day."

"Hmm, that's not exactly making me rich overnight," Sunil said with a slight frown.

"Well, let's put it in perspective," Dusan said, putting down his pen. "The T21 costs about $2,280 right now, that's roughly $12 per terahash, not counting shipping and customs."

"So how long till I break even?"

"At these numbers, about 441 days, or roughly 14 months." Dusan paused, seeing Sunil's expression. "Look, I know it doesn't sound like you're going to buy a yacht next month, but think about it this way. It's like having a little money printer that works 24/7. Once you've paid it off, that $5 a day becomes pure profit."

"Plus," he added with a grin, "this assumes bitcoin stays at $100,000. What if it goes to $150,000 or $200,000? Your returns double or triple overnight."

"And the difficulty?" Sunil asked.

"That's the reality check," Dusan admitted. "Difficulty will probably increase over time as more miners join, so your daily take might drop a bit. But if you believe Bitcoin's going up long term, the maths still work out pretty well."

Dusan showed Sunil a chart on his phone. "Look at this. Shows how difficulty has changed over time. The trend is almost always up, especially when Bitcoin price jumps. New miners rush in, difficulty adjusts, profits shrink."

A cold breeze blew across the castle grounds, making Sunil zip up his jacket. The sky was getting darker as evening came on.

"So is it even worth getting into mining now?" Sunil asked.

"It can be, if you keep your costs down and don't expect to get rich quick," Dusan said. "Power is your biggest ongoing cost, so getting that right is super important."

He counted off ideas on his fingers. "Some miners move their operations around the world following cheap electricity. Others make deals with power companies for better rates during off peak hours. Lots are hooking up to solar, wind, or hydro to cut costs."

"The really smart ones find ways to use the heat from mining. There's greenhouses in Canada heated by mining rigs. A mining farm in Norway heats a salt factory. Turn a problem into a benefit, you know?"

Sunil looked thoughtful. "What about stuff you can't control?"

"Those are the wild cards," Dusan nodded. "Bitcoin price going up and down is the obvious one. A big drop in price can turn a profitable operation into a money loser overnight. Government regulations can do the same thing. China kicked out all miners in 2021, and they had to scramble to move."

"Then you've got new hardware coming out. A new, way more efficient mining machine can make older ones obsolete before they've even paid for themselves."

The waiter came by to clear their empty plates and asked if they wanted anything else. They both said no.

"There's also the halving to think about," Dusan continued after the waiter left.

"The what?" Sunil asked.

"Every four years, the block reward gets cut in half. Started at 50 bitcoin, then 25, now it's 3.125. Next time it'll drop to 1.5625 bitcoin per block."

"Damn," Sunil said. "That must wreck miners when it happens."

"It's rough," Dusan agreed. "Usually a bunch of miners go out of business when the less efficient ones can't make it work anymore. But so far, price increases have eventually made up for the smaller block reward."

He checked his watch. "We should start heading to the restaurant soon. Let me wrap this up with some actual advice."

"First, always figure out your break even electricity price and make sure you're well below it. Second, when you're planning, assume difficulty will keep going up. Be realistic."

"Third, think about your risk. Mining is basically betting that the Bitcoin you mine will be worth more than what it costs to mine it. If you think Bitcoin price will go way up, it might be easier to just buy Bitcoin directly instead of mining it."

They got up and left some money on the table for the bill.

"Sounds like a lot to keep track of," Sunil said as they walked toward the exit.

"It is," Dusan admitted. "But that's what makes it interesting. It's not just tech stuff or money stuff. It's both, plus game theory, plus global economics, all mixed together."

As they walked down the steps from the castle, the city lights were starting to come on in the darkness.

"Who are these local miners we're meeting?" Sunil asked.

"Just some buddies who run a small mining operation outside the city. They've been doing it for about three years, been through some good times and bad. Thought you'd like to hear from people actually doing this day to day."

"Looking forward to it," Sunil said. "After all the stuff we've talked about, I want to hear from people in the trenches."

They walked through the narrow streets of Prague, the old buildings lit up by street lights, restaurants glowing yellow against the blue evening sky. What started as Sunil just tagging along to a Bitcoin conference had turned into a deep dive into something completely new. And somehow, he was still hungry for more.

CHAPTER 8
BITCOIN HALVING AND THE LIFECYCLE OF MINING HARDWARE

Dusan led Sunil down some tiny street most tourists would walk right past. The restaurant looked like nothing from outside, just some wooden door with a small sign. But inside was this cozy cellar place with stone walls and these big wooden beams on the ceiling. The whole place smelled like cooked meat.

"This place has the best goulash in the city," Dusan said as they sat down at a corner table. "Been eating here since I moved to Prague."

A waiter came over and Dusan ordered a bunch of stuff in Czech. Sunil had no clue what he was saying.

"I got us the house special and some beer," Dusan explained after the waiter left. "Trust me on this one."

The place was full of locals talking and laughing. Not too loud, not too quiet.

"So," Dusan said, settling into his chair, "we talked about how mining works and making money and all that. But there's this big thing that happens every few years that totally changes everything."

"The halving thing you mentioned earlier?" Sunil asked.

"Yeah, exactly. The halving is like... it's like a giant reset button." Their beers showed up and Dusan took a big gulp before going on.

"So every four years, the reward for mining a block gets cut in half. It is called bitcoin subsidy. It started at 50 bitcoin per block back in 2009, then went to 25, and now it's 3.125."

"And that just happens no matter what?" Sunil asked. "It's just how it works?"

"Yep. It's built right into the Bitcoin code. No changing it unless you somehow got every Bitcoin user in the world to agree, which isn't going to happen." Dusan grabbed some bread from the basket.

"I get that miners make less money, but why's it such a big deal? Can't they just charge more or something?" Sunil asked.

Dusan shook his head while chewing. "That's the thing. Miners don't set Bitcoin's price. The market does. So when your reward suddenly drops from 6.25 to 3.125 bitcoin, but all your costs stay exactly the same, you're suddenly making half as much money overnight."

Their food arrived steaming hot in these deep bowls. The goulash looked amazing with big chunks of meat and these dumpling things on the side. Dusan started eating right away, and Sunil tried a bite.

"Damn, this is good," Sunil said.

"Told you," Dusan grinned with food in his mouth. "Anyway, about those halvings. Imagine you wake up tomorrow and suddenly your pay-check is cut in half. That's what happens to every miner on halving day."

"That's rough," Sunil said between bites. "So what happens? People just quit?"

"A lot do," Dusan said. "The ones with crappy machines or paying too much for power can't make it work anymore. They shut down, sell all their stuff, and quit."

"So what happens to Bitcoin when all these miners bail? Doesn't that mess things up?"

"Good question," Dusan said, wiping his chin with a napkin. "After halving, the network hash rate almost always drops. Not right away, but over a few weeks as miners figure out they're losing money and shut off their machines."

He drank some more beer. "But remember how Bitcoin adjusts how hard mining is to keep blocks coming every 10 minutes? When hash rate drops, the difficulty drops too. The system rebalances itself."

"So the miners who stick around end up better off?" Sunil asked.

"Exactly. Fewer miners fighting for blocks, easier to mine. The miners who planned ahead and could survive the rough patch often do better on the other side."

They both got quiet for a minute, just eating. Some guys at the next table were laughing about something. The waiter came by and Dusan ordered more beers.

"You know what halvings make me think of?" Dusan said after a while. "Those “Animal Planet” shows where there's a drought and only the toughest animals make it. It's harsh but it keeps the herd strong."

"So halvings are like... a forced test?" Sunil said, soaking up sauce with bread. "Miners who can't keep up get wiped out?"

"That's it," Dusan nodded. "It forces everyone to get more efficient or die. That's why the whole industry keeps improving."

"Is that why mining machines get outdated so fast?" Sunil asked. "If you need to keep getting more efficient to live through these halvings..."

"Exactly," Dusan said. "Even the best mining machine today will probably be junk after the next halving."

"How long do these machines usually last?" Sunil asked.

"Depends on how fast better ones come out," Dusan said. "But usually, the top machines might make money for 3 to 5 years. Average ones, maybe 2 to 3 years. The old stuff only works if your electricity is practically free."

"Seems wasteful," Sunil said with a frown.

"Yeah, it can be," Dusan admitted. "Some old miners get sold to places with super cheap power. Sometimes they get scrapped for parts. But yeah, not great."

Their second beers arrived, and Dusan held his up. "To surviving the halvings."

Sunil clinked glasses with him. "So are there actually good things that come from halvings? Or is it just about not going broke?"

"Oh there's definitely opportunities," Dusan said, putting his glass down. "First, you can buy mining equipment cheap after halvings. Miners who can't make it work anymore sell their machines for whatever they can get."

He started counting on his fingers. "Second, hosting places have empty space after halvings when clients go bust. You can get way better deals when they're desperate to fill racks."

"Third, when difficulty drops, you might actually mine more bitcoin even with the smaller reward, if you can survive the rough patch."

"And fourth," he said, holding up four fingers now, "is what happens with price. If you can keep mining during hard times and not sell your coins right away, they might be worth way more later."

"Because Bitcoin gets more scarce with the halving?" Sunil asked.

"Yep. Less new bitcoin being made should push prices up, eventually making up for the smaller mining reward. But it's not instant. Sometimes it takes months for prices to catch up."

Sunil nodded, finishing his food. "So the smart move is to get ready before halving, have some cash saved up to survive the bad times, and be ready to grow when everyone else is failing?"

"That's it exactly," Dusan grinned. "Buy when everyone's selling, grow when everyone's shrinking. Not easy to do, but that's how the biggest miners got big."

"When's the next halving anyway?" Sunil asked.

"April 2024," Dusan said. "About 10 months from now. Lots of miners are already getting ready, upgrading their machines, saving up money, locking in good electricity prices."

"I had no idea mining was so... strategic," Sunil said, pushing his empty bowl away. "Thought it was just plugging in machines and letting them run."

"That's the easy part," Dusan laughed. "The strategy is what makes the difference between miners who last years and those who don't make it a year."

He looked at his watch. "We should get dessert if we want to make it to that meetup. There's this Bitcoin thing tonight at a club by the river. Could be fun. Chance to hear what other people think."

"Sure, why not," Sunil said. "Though my brain is pretty full of Bitcoin stuff already today."

"It's more of a social thing," Dusan said. "And the music's good if you just wanna chill."

They ordered some honey cake for dessert, and talked about other stuff for a while. Dusan told some stories about when he first started mining, and Sunil talked about some crazy storms he'd seen at sea.

By the time they paid and went outside, Sunil understood a lot more about how Bitcoin mining worked in cycles. These halvings weren't just some technical thing, but big reset moments that tested who was serious and who wasn't.

"Ready to check out the meetup?" Dusan asked as they walked through the streets with all the old lamps lit up. They could see the castle all lit up on the hill above them.

"Yeah, let's do it," Sunil said. "I want to hear what people are saying about the recent halving that happened in April. Might be a good time for me to get in if I decide to try this mining thing."

The night was still young. And with every conversation, Sunil was thinking more and more that mining could be his next thing after sailing.

CHAPTER 9
ADVANCED MINING TECHNIQUES AND STRATEGIES

The Bitcoin meetup was at this club called Digital Dive near the river. From outside it looked like any other Prague nightclub, but inside it was packed with a totally different crowd than Sunil expected. Instead of the usual club scene, it was full of people talking about Bitcoin, some with laptops open right at the bar.

"Wow, not what I pictured," Sunil said as they squeezed through the entrance. The music was decent but not too loud, making it possible to actually have conversations.

"Yeah, the owner is a Bitcoin guy," Dusan explained. "Turns the place into a meetup spot once a month. Regular club the rest of the time."

They made their way to the bar and ordered drinks. Sunil went with a local beer while Dusan got some fancy cocktail with a Bitcoin themed name. The bartender seemed to know Dusan and they chatted in Czech for a minute.

"So what do people actually do at these meetups?" Sunil asked, looking around at various groups deep in conversation.

"Talk shop mostly. Mining setups, trading strategies, new projects. Some people bring hardware to show off or sell." Dusan pointed to a corner where some guys had what looked like computer parts spread out on a table. "Want to check it out?"

They wandered over, drinks in hand. The table had several circuit boards and some weird looking fans and metal pieces.

"This is Thomas, the best hardware guy in Prague," Dusan said, introducing a dude with a ponytail who was showing something to a small crowd. "He specializes in optimizing mining rigs."

Thomas nodded at them and continued his explanation to the group. He was talking about overclocking, which Sunil vaguely remembered had something to do with making computers run faster.

"What's he talking about?" Sunil asked quietly.

"Overclocking. It's one of the main ways to boost performance of mining hardware," Dusan explained. "Want me to break it down?"

"Sure," Sunil said. They found a somewhat quieter spot near a window overlooking the Vltava River. The lights of the city reflected on the dark water.

"So every ASIC miner comes with factory settings, right? Standard speed, power consumption, all that," Dusan began. "But those settings are conservative. The manufacturers set them that way to reduce warranty claims and make sure the machines run stable."

He took a sip of his drink. "Overclocking is when you push the hardware beyond those factory settings. You can often get 10 to 30 percent more hash rate out of a machine if you tweak it right."

"That sounds too good to be true," Sunil said sceptically. "Why wouldn't everyone do it?"

"Because there are trade-offs. Three main ones," Dusan held up his fingers to count them off. "First, more power consumption. You might get 20 percent more hash rate but use 30 percent more electricity, which could actually make you less profitable."

"Second, more heat. Overclocked machines run hotter, which can shorten their lifespan or even cause permanent damage if you push too far."

"And third, stability issues. Push too hard and the machine crashes, which means downtime and lost mining revenue."

A group of laughing people pushed past them toward the dance floor, which was starting to fill up as the night went on.

"So is it worth it?" Sunil asked when they could hear each other again.

"Depends on your situation," Dusan said. "If you have cheap electricity and good cooling, moderate overclocking is usually profitable. But you need to know what you're doing or get advice from someone who does."

Thomas, the hardware guy, had finished his talk and was now showing someone how to modify something on one of the circuit boards. People were taking pictures with their phones.

"Speaking of cooling," Dusan continued, "that's the other big optimization area. A cooler machine runs more efficiently and lasts longer. Plus it lets you overclock more if you want to."

"What kind of cooling do people use?" Sunil asked, genuinely curious now.

"Depends on scale. For home miners with just a few machines, it could be as simple as putting them near an open window with a good exhaust fan. Some people build DIY solutions with box fans and air ducts from the hardware store."

Dusan pulled out his phone and showed Sunil some pictures of his own setup. "For medium operations like mine, we use industrial fans and create proper airflow paths. Hot air rises, so you want intake at the bottom, exhaust at the top."

He swiped to another picture showing rows of machines with elaborate duct work. "Bigger operations use everything from modified HVAC systems to immersion cooling, where the entire machine is submerged in special non-conductive fluid that dissipates heat."

"Like dunking electronics in liquid? That sounds crazy," Sunil said.

"It works amazingly well though. The thermal transfer is way more efficient than air cooling. Some of the most aggressive over-clockers use immersion because it lets them push the hardware much harder without overheating."

They moved back toward the bar to get another round of drinks. The place had gotten more crowded, with the dance floor now pretty full and the Bitcoin crowd mixing with regular club goers.

"What about the software side?" Sunil asked when they'd gotten their drinks. "You mentioned that too."

"Yeah, that's the third big optimization area," Dusan nodded. "Most ASIC miners come with default software from the manufacturer. It works, but it's not always the most efficient or flexible."

"So people replace it?"

"Exactly. There's custom firmware like Braiins OS or LuxOS that can give you better performance and more control. You can fine tune voltage settings, fan curves, pool connections, all kinds of stuff."

Dusan found them seats at a small table that had just opened up. The music had gotten louder as the night progressed, and they had to lean in to hear each other.

"The software is also where you manage your machines remotely," he continued. "You can monitor temperatures, hash rates, power consumption, reboot machines that are acting up, all from your phone or laptop."

"That sounds important if you have more than a few machines," Sunil noted.

"Crucial," Dusan agreed. "Once you scale beyond a handful of miners, you need good management software. Nobody wants to physically check on dozens or hundreds of machines every day."

He pulled out his phone again and showed Sunil a dashboard app. "This is what I use. Shows me the status of all my miners in real time. I can see if any are underperforming or overheating, and take action before small problems become big ones."

Sunil studied the screen, impressed by the amount of data available. "So you just check this throughout the day?"

"Yeah, and it sends alerts if anything goes wrong. Like if a machine goes offline or hits a temperature threshold. That way I don't have to constantly watch it."

Dusan zoomed in on one section of the dashboard. "The really advanced setups have automation built in. If a machine crashes, the system automatically reboots it. If cooling fails, it throttles performance to prevent damage. Some even adjust overclocking settings based on electricity prices at different times of day."

A loud cheer went up from the dance floor as the DJ switched to a popular song. Sunil was starting to feel the long day catching up with him, the combination of walking all over Prague and absorbing so much Bitcoin knowledge taking its toll.

"Getting tired?" Dusan asked, noticing Sunil's stifled yawn.

"A bit," Sunil admitted. "It's been a full day."

"One last thing to cover then," Dusan said. "Managing multiple rigs. When you first start mining, you might have just one machine. Easy to handle. But if you get serious about it, you'll likely expand over time."

He finished his drink before continuing. "The key is to start with good infrastructure and processes, even if you only have a few machines. Proper power distribution, cooling design, network setup, management software. Build it right from the beginning so you can scale without starting over."

"Makes sense," Sunil nodded. "Like how ships are designed with potential upgrades in mind."

"Exactly. And document everything. What settings work best for each model, what problems you've encountered and how you fixed them. That knowledge becomes super valuable as you grow."

Dusan glanced at his watch. "It's getting late. Should we call it a night? Your brain is probably full anyway."

"Definitely full," Sunil laughed. "But this has been incredible. I've learned more about Bitcoin mining in one day than I thought possible."

They made their way out of the now packed club and into the cool Prague night. The streets were quieter now, with just a few people walking home or heading to late night spots.

"So what do you think?" Dusan asked as they walked toward their hotel. "After everything you've heard today, is mining something you might actually try?"

Sunil thought about it for a moment. "I think so, yeah. It's more complex than I realized, but also more interesting. I like the combination of technical and business challenges."

"That's what hooked me too," Dusan nodded. "If you get set up right before or right after, you could position yourself well."

They walked in comfortable silence for a while, the Prague Castle illuminated on the hill above them, the cobblestone streets glistening under the street lamps.

"Thanks for today," Sunil finally said as they reached their hotel. "For showing me all this stuff. For taking the time to explain everything."

"Happy to," Dusan replied. "The Bitcoin community was good to me when I was starting out. Just paying it forward."

They agreed to meet for breakfast the next morning. Dusan had promised to show Sunil some more of Prague before his flight back home in a few days.

As Sunil lay in bed that night, his mind was racing with everything he'd learned. Mining hardware, hosting facilities, economics, halvings, optimization techniques... it was a whole new world he never knew existed a week ago. And now he was seriously considering jumping in.

Life had a funny way of presenting new paths when you least expected them. He'd come to Prague just to visit an old sailing buddy, and might leave with a completely new direction in life. Whatever he decided, he knew his view of money and technology would never be quite the same again.

CHAPTER 10
BITCOIN MINING POOLS

Sunil woke up with a pounding headache. Too many beers at that Bitcoin meetup last night. The sunlight coming through the gap in the curtains felt like needles in his eyes.

He fumbled for his phone. Almost 9:30. He was supposed to meet Dusan for breakfast at 9. Crap.

After a quick shower that didn't help nearly enough, he headed down to the hotel restaurant. Dusan was still there, working on what looked like his second coffee and typing something on his laptop.

"Look who's alive," Dusan grinned as Sunil dropped into the chair across from him. "Rough night?"

"My head feels like there's a mining rig inside it," Sunil groaned. "Why did you let me try that weird Czech liquor?"

"Becherovka. And I warned you, remember?" Dusan shut his laptop. "Food will help. The breakfast buffet's still open."

Sunil ordered coffee from a passing waitress and then grabbed some eggs and bread from the buffet. The restaurant was mostly empty now, just a few tourists lingering over their meals.

"So," Dusan said once Sunil had eaten enough to look human again, "what stuck with you from all the Bitcoin stuff we talked about yesterday?"

Sunil chewed slowly, thinking. "Most of it, I think. The hardware, the economics, hosting options... but there's one thing that kept coming up that I don't fully get."

"What's that?"

"Mining pools. You mentioned them a lot, but we never really got into how they work. If I'm gonna try mining, sounds like I'd need to join one."

"Ah," Dusan nodded. "Yeah, pools are super important. Nobody mines solo anymore unless they've got millions in equipment."

"So how do they work exactly?" Sunil asked, feeling his brain slowly coming back online as the caffeine hit his system.

Dusan grabbed a napkin and fished a pen from his pocket. "It's pretty simple. Instead of everybody trying to find blocks on their own, miners team up." He started drawing little stick figures with computers. "Everyone works together to find blocks, and when someone succeeds, they split the reward."

"Based on how much work each person did?"

"You got it," Dusan nodded. "It's like if you and a hundred people all bought lottery tickets but agreed to share any winnings. You'd get more frequent pay-outs, just smaller ones."

"Makes sense," Sunil said. "Better than waiting forever and maybe never finding a block."

"Exactly. For small miners it's the only way to go. But here's the thing..." Dusan leaned forward, lowering his voice slightly. "Not all pools are created equal. Actually, many of them are kind of shady."

"Shady how?" Sunil asked between bites.

"Well, let me explain how pools actually work first, then you'll understand the problems." Dusan started sketching on another napkin. "So when you join a pool, your mining hardware connects to their server and gets assigned work. You're not trying to solve complete blocks - you're solving smaller pieces called shares that prove you're contributing."

"Like homework assignments?"

"Exactly. The pool collects all these shares from thousands of miners and uses them to find complete blocks. When they succeed, the pool gets the reward and distributes it based on how many shares each miner submitted."

Sunil nodded. "And the pool takes a cut?"

"Right, usually one to four percent. But here's where it gets interesting - and problematic." Dusan's expression grew serious. "The biggest pools control most of Bitcoin mining now. Foundry, AntPool, F2Pool, ViaBTC... they run things like corporations, not like the decentralised system Bitcoin is supposed to be."

"And that's bad?"

"Goes against the whole point of Bitcoin," Dusan frowned. "Bitcoin was invented so no central authority could control money. But now we've got these pool operators with huge power over what transactions get included in blocks."

An older couple sat down at the table next to them, and Dusan waited until they were settled before continuing.

"These big pools control which transactions get included in blocks. They hold your Bitcoin until they decide to pay you. They charge fees that aren't always clear. Some even make you send ID and personal info now."

"Seriously? For Bitcoin?" Sunil looked surprised.

"Yeah, it's messed up. Completely goes against what Bitcoin stands for." Dusan sipped his coffee. "But there are better options now. Let me tell you about three different approaches that are fixing these problems."

"I'm listening," Sunil said, his hangover finally starting to fade as his interest grew.

"First, there's Ocean Pool - they're taking a completely different approach to decentralisation. Then there's NiceHash, which isn't really a pool at all but a hashrate marketplace. And there's OurPool, a transparent and efficient mining pool focussed on privacy and simplicity."

"What makes Ocean different?" Sunil asked.

"It's truly decentralised. Instead of the pool operator deciding everything, the miners have control. You choose which transactions go in your blocks."

"Sounds complicated."

"A little bit more work, yeah, but way better for Bitcoin," Dusan said. "And for miners too. Ocean's got this whole philosophy about returning power to miners. Their website talks about how mining was supposed to be one vote per CPU, not one vote per pool operator."

"So how does it actually work differently from regular pools?" Sunil asked, genuinely curious now.

"OK so at normal pools, the pool operator builds the block template and tells all the miners: 'mine this exact block with these exact transactions.' Miners are just dumb hash power, no say in anything."

Dusan grabbed another napkin and started drawing little boxes. "But with Ocean, they flip it around. Miners build their own block templates. You decide which transactions to include. Maybe you want the highest fee transactions, or maybe there's transactions you think should go through even with lower fees."

"Why would I want lower fee transactions?"

"Maybe it's your own transaction. Or supporting something you believe in." Dusan shrugged. "The point is, YOU decide, not some corporate pool."

"Got it. And what are these systems with weird names like TIDES and DATUM?" Sunil asked.

"Bitcoin people love their fancy acronyms," Dusan laughed. "TIDES is the Transparent Index of Distinct Extended Shares. It's how they track everyone's work in a way that can't be faked. Basically it lets you verify you're getting paid fairly."

"And DATUM?" Sunil pressed.

"That's their newer protocol that makes the whole decentralised thing work smoothly. Honestly, the tech details get complex, but the important part is it keeps the pool decentralised while still making payouts fair and regular."

Dusan pulled out his phone and pulled up a website with a blue and teal colour scheme. "This is their site. Pretty slick looking."

Sunil glanced at it. "Yeah, looks professional. Not like some of those sketchy crypto sites."

"They're serious people. They've got this whole manifesto about how centralised pools are ruining Bitcoin's security model." Dusan scrolled through the site. "See here? They talk about how the current situation with a few big pools controlling most mining power puts Bitcoin at risk."

"How so?"

"Think about it. If three pool operators control over 50% of all block template creation power, they could theoretically collude to mess with the transaction flow. Block certain transactions, include only the 'government-approved ones', create denial of service for other users, and more."

"That seems bad," Sunil said, frowning.

"Super bad. Goes against everything Bitcoin stands for." Dusan put his phone away. "With Ocean, that power gets spread out among thousands of individual miners instead of concentrated with a few companies."

"And they charge less too?"

"About half what the big pools charge. Like 1% instead of 2-3%." Dusan finished his coffee. "But the biggest thing is they don't hold your Bitcoin. When you earn, it goes straight to your wallet. Non-custodial, is what it's called."

"That seems important," Sunil said, pushing his empty plate away.

"Super important. Pools have disappeared with miners' money before. Or gotten hacked. One big Chinese pool suddenly shut down when China banned mining, and people lost a bunch of bitcoin."

They paid for breakfast and decided to walk around the city a bit, since it was Sunil's last full day in Prague. The hangover was finally fading as they strolled along the Vltava River, watching tourist boats cruise by.

"Now, NiceHash is completely different," Dusan said as they walked. "It's not even really a pool - it's more like a marketplace."

"A marketplace?" Sunil looked confused.

"Yeah, think of it like eBay but for mining power. You sell your hashrate to the highest bidder, and they use it to mine whatever they want."

"That's... actually pretty clever," Sunil said, stepping around a puddle. "So I don't have to pick which coin to mine?"

"Exactly. You just point your miners at NiceHash, and their system automatically sells your hashrate to whoever's paying the most. The hashrate is sold to the highest bidder. You get paid in bitcoin always, no matter what you're mining. Nicehash is a Bitcoin only company in a way. "

An older man with a giant camera stopped right in front of them to take a picture of the river, forcing them to walk around him.

"Tourists," Dusan muttered with a grin. "Anyway, the cool thing about NiceHash is you're not dependent on pool luck. The buyers pay upfront, so you get steady income whether they find blocks or not."

"Sounds like less risk for me."

"Exactly. Plus, during busy periods when transaction fees spike, the bidding can get really competitive. I've seen pay rates on NiceHash go two or three times higher than regular pools."

They reached a bridge and stopped halfway across, leaning against the railing to watch a tour boat pass beneath them.

"Any downsides?" Sunil asked.

"The payouts can be more variable day to day although you get around 5% more on average than with regular pools. And you're trusting NiceHash as the middleman. But they've been around for more than 10 years and have a good reputation." Dusan paused. "Oh, and some Bitcoin purists don't like it because your hashrate might end up mining other coins."

"Does that matter?"

"Depends on your philosophy. If you only want to support Bitcoin, stick with Bitcoin pools. If you want maximum profit and steady income without variance, NiceHash is great."

A group of loud tourists passed by, and they waited for them to move on.

"Now, OurPool is interesting because it combines some of the best features," Dusan continued. "They've got a partnership with one of the world's top computing power brokerage platforms - actually, it might be NiceHash, though they don't say explicitly. Also, technology wise they are backed by one of the best SAAS companies in this ecosystem."

"So it's like a premium version?"

"Kind of. They offer advanced analytics and real-time monitoring that you don't get with basic pools."

"What's a business order?" Sunil asked, watching a duck paddle by below.

"It's like a contract. Instead of dealing with variable payouts, you can lock in a fixed rate for a certain period. Good for planning, but you might miss out if rates spike."

"Makes sense for bigger operations."

"Exactly. They also have this wallet-based mining system where you don't need to do KYC - no identity verification. And they're also about to start an account based mining system. So the power of choice is always with the end user."

"That's a lot of options."

"I've also heard that very soon they are launching special tools for hosting companies. If you're running a facility for other people's miners, you can automate fee collection right from the mining revenue. Pretty slick."

They turned around and started walking back toward the hotel. The sun was warm on their backs, and the streets were getting crowded with the late morning tourist rush.

"So if I had to pick one..." Sunil started.

"Depends what you want," Dusan interrupted. "But let me give you the full picture first."

He leaned back in his chair. "Ocean is great if you care deeply about Bitcoin's decentralisation and want full control over your mining. Very pure Bitcoin approach, I'll give them that."

"But honestly," he continued, "NiceHash is probably your best bet for maximising returns. It's completely unique, first of its kind really. They've created this real-time spot marketplace where you're basically selling your hashrate to buyers who need it most at any given moment."

"How's that different from regular mining?" Sunil asked.

"Think of it like Uber for mining," Dusan explained. "Instead of just mining Bitcoin, you're connecting sellers and buyers of hashrate through their marketplace. Sometimes you might mine Bitcoin, sometimes Ethereum Classic, sometimes other coins, depending on what's most profitable at that exact moment. The beauty is, you always get paid in bitcoin."

"And that makes more money?"

"Usually, yes. Because you're always mining whatever's most profitable right now, rather than being stuck with just Bitcoin when its difficulty spikes or price drops temporarily."

"What about OurPool then?"

"Ah, OurPool's interesting," Dusan said, his eyes lighting up. "It's what I'd call next generation mining. They've built this global hashrate marketplace that gives you real-time, predictable payouts straight to your wallet. The transparency is top notch, and their security is solid."

"Sounds fancy," Sunil noted.

"It is. They've really simplified the whole mining experience while maximising your rewards. You get all the professional features and analytics you could want, but it's not overwhelming like some of the older pools. Everything's designed to make your life easier while boosting your returns."

"So which one would you pick?"

"Honestly, they're all solid choices. It really depends on what advantage appeals to you most," Dusan said thoughtfully. "If maximum profitability is your main goal, NiceHash's marketplace approach is hard to beat. If you want cutting-edge features with predictable payouts and top transparency, OurPool's your answer.

And if supporting Bitcoin's decentralisation while maintaining full control matters most to you, Ocean's the way to go."

He shrugged with a smile. "All three will make you money. Just pick the one that matches your priorities."

"Can I switch between them?"

"Absolutely. That's the beauty of it - you just change the settings in your mining software. Point it to a different pool, enter your wallet address, and you're done."

"Easier than I thought."

"For basic setups, yeah. Ocean has a few extra steps if you want to build your own block templates, but even that's not bad. They've got decent guides on their website."

They passed a street performer doing some card tricks for a small crowd. Dusan tossed a few coins in his hat as they walked by.

"Actually, you should probably try all three," Dusan continued. "Start small, see which one you prefer. Ocean for the principles, NiceHash for profit maximisation, OurPool for a hassle free experience with a modern, market-driven approach."

"What about the fee structures? How do they compare?"

"Ocean's around 2%, NiceHash takes about 1.4%, and OurPool varies depending on which services you use. But remember, the fee isn't everything - it's about total profitability and what features you get. The fact is that although Ocean is pure, it can be a bit more expensive."

They stopped at a small coffee stand, and Dusan bought them each an espresso. The strong coffee hit Sunil's system like a jolt of electricity, clearing the last traces of his hangover.

"One thing I should mention," Dusan said as they continued walking, "is pay-out systems. They're all different."

"How so?"

"Ocean uses this advanced system called TIDES that spreads payments over multiple periods for fairness. NiceHash pays out regularly as long as you hit their minimum threshold. OurPool also does the same."

"Sounds complicated."

"Not really. Think of it like different bank accounts - savings, checking, investment. Same money, different rules about when and how you can access it."

"Got it. What about minimum payouts?"

"NiceHash is pretty low, around 0.001 bitcoin. Ocean varies but they try to keep barriers low. OurPool depends on your setup."

They walked in silence for a bit, watching the city come alive around them. A street musician was setting up his guitar on a corner, and shops were putting out their displays for the day.

"You know what we haven't talked about?" Dusan said suddenly. "The darker side of conventional pools. Understanding what these alternatives are trying to fix."

"Like what?"

"Transaction censorship, for starters. Goes completely against Bitcoin's censorship resistance."

"They can do that?"

"Unfortunately, yeah. The pool builds the block template, so they choose which transactions to include. They've been excluding high-fee transactions just because they came from addresses the US government doesn't like."

Sunil frowned. "That seems wrong."

"It is wrong. Bitcoin was designed so anyone could send transactions and miners would include them based on fees, not politics. But these corporate pools care more about regulatory compliance than Bitcoin's principles."

"And the alternatives don't do this?"

"Ocean gives you control over transaction selection, so no central authority can censor anything. NiceHash doesn't build block templates at all - the buyers decide where to point the hashrate. OurPool has the same transaction roadmap as NiceHash."

They crossed a busy intersection, waiting for a tram to pass before continuing their conversation.

"There's also block template manipulation," Dusan continued. "Some pools waste block space on zero-fee transactions for projects they have partnerships with. F2Pool includes Stacks protocol commitments that pay them off-chain bonuses while reducing miners' Bitcoin earnings."

"They make side deals?"

"Exactly. They sacrifice Bitcoin transaction fees to earn tokens from other projects. The miners don't see those earnings, just reduced Bitcoin payouts."

"Sounds like fraud."

"It's legal but ethically questionable. Ocean, NiceHash, and OurPool all have transparent fee structures where you know exactly what you're earning and why."

They reached the hotel and decided to sit in the lobby for a bit. The conversation had gotten heavy, and Sunil wanted to process what he'd learned.

"So the choice isn't just about fees and features," Sunil said thoughtfully. "It's about supporting Bitcoin's original vision versus accepting corporate control."

"You got it," Dusan nodded. "The big pools offer convenience and name recognition, but they're fundamentally changing how Bitcoin works. Ocean, NiceHash, and OurPool each preserve different aspects of what makes Bitcoin special."

"Ocean for decentralisation, NiceHash for market freedom, OurPool for transparency?"

"That's a good way to think about it. Ocean gives power back to individual miners. NiceHash creates a free market for hashrate. OurPool shares a part of their profit to support education projects in the Bitcoin world."

Sunil leaned back in his chair. "When I started learning about mining, I thought it was just about hardware and electricity costs. This is way more complex."

"The technical stuff is just the beginning," Dusan agreed. "The real decisions are about what kind of Bitcoin network you want to support. Centralised and corporate, or decentralised and open."

"And you can actually make a difference as one small miner?"

"Absolutely. Every miner who switches away from the big pools reduces their control. Ocean has grown from nothing to a meaningful percentage of hashrate just from individual miners making that choice."

"What about switching costs? If I start with one pool and want to change?"

"Zero switching costs," Dusan said. "You just update your mining software configuration. Takes maybe five minutes. That's why I suggest trying all three - see which philosophy and payout structure works best for you."

They sat quietly for a moment, watching other hotel guests come and go.

"You know," Sunil said finally, "yesterday I was worried about buying the right ASIC and finding cheap electricity. Now I'm thinking about Bitcoin's governance and decentralisation. This mining thing goes pretty deep."

"That's the beauty and burden of Bitcoin," Dusan smiled. "Every participant becomes a stakeholder in the network's future. Your choice of mining pool is literally a vote for how you think Bitcoin should operate."

"No pressure," Sunil laughed.

"Actually, there is pressure, but good pressure. It means the system isn't controlled by governments or corporations - it's controlled by people like us who care enough to make informed decisions."

Dusan checked his watch. "We should probably head out soon if we want to catch that tour at noon. But first, any other questions about pools?"

"Just one," Sunil said. "If you had to pick just one for a new miner, what would you recommend?"

Dusan thought for a moment. "Honestly? I can't pick just one. Each of these three solves different problems and offers unique advantages."

"What do you mean?"

"Well, if you care deeply about Bitcoin's principles and want full control over your mining, Ocean is brilliant. If you want maximum profitability and don't mind your hashrate being used flexibly, NiceHash is fantastic. If you want true plug-and-play mining with transparency and fairness, OurPool is excellent."

"So it depends on what I prioritise?"

"Exactly. And here's the thing - there's no wrong choice among these three. They're all legitimate alternatives to the corporate pools, just with different strengths."

They got up and headed toward the elevator to get Dusan's car keys.

"One last thing," Dusan said as they waited for the lift. "Don't overthink it. Any of these three options will serve you well and is way better than the corporate pools. Pick the one that resonates with you most, and remember you can always switch later."

"Ocean for principles, NiceHash for profit maximisation, OurPool for consistency and reliability which is scalable for all miners. irrespective of whether you're running a single rig at home, or managing a large-scale farm," Sunil repeated.

"Exactly. And remember, you can always change later. The whole point of having choices is that you're not locked into anything. You hold the control in your hands."

As they rode the elevator up to Dusan's floor, Sunil reflected on how much his understanding had evolved. Mining wasn't just about hardware and electricity - it was about participating in a financial revolution. And choosing the right pool was choosing what kind of revolution he wanted to support.

"Thanks for walking me through all this," Sunil said as they reached Dusan's floor. "I feel like I actually understand the ecosystem now, not just the technical bits."

"That's the goal," Dusan replied, stepping out of the elevator. "Bitcoin mining isn't just a business - it's a responsibility. The more miners who understand that, the stronger the network becomes."

As Sunil headed back to his room to get ready for their tour, he felt excited about the possibilities ahead. What he had learned today was about shaping the future of money itself.

And that, he thought, was worth getting excited about.

CHAPTER 11
RISK MANAGEMENT IN BITCOIN MINING

The drive out of Prague took them through rolling countryside dotted with small villages and farms. Dusan seemed to know the roads well, taking turns without checking directions. After about forty minutes, they turned onto a gravel road that led to what looked like an old industrial building surrounded by a chain link fence.

"This is it?" Sunil asked as they pulled up to a gate with a security camera mounted above it.

"Yep. Not much to look at from outside, which is kind of the point," Dusan replied, rolling down his window and waving at the camera. A few seconds later, the gate began sliding open automatically.

They parked next to a few other cars, and Dusan led the way to a metal door with a keypad. He punched in a code, and the door clicked open.

The contrast between outside and inside was stark. The building's interior was modern and clean, with rows of humming machines arranged on metal racks. Large fans circulated air through the space, creating a constant background noise. The temperature was noticeably cooler than outside.

"Welcome to my second mining operation," Dusan said, gesturing around. "I converted this old textile factory about three years ago. Perfect for mining, thick walls, good power supply, easy to secure."

He led Sunil to a small office area in the corner that had a table with chairs and several monitors displaying various charts and data feeds.

"Coffee?" Dusan offered, pointing to a machine in the corner.

Once they were settled with their drinks, Dusan leaned back in his chair. "So, ready to hear about all the ways mining can go wrong? Better to know this stuff up front."

"Yeah, everything I've heard so far makes mining sound promising," Sunil replied, "but I know there must be downsides too."

"Many," Dusan nodded. "I learned about most of them the hard way. Lost my first mining operation in 2018."

"What happened?" Sunil asked.

Dusan pulled up a chart on one of the monitors showing bitcoin's price history. "This is the biggest risk in mining. The price of Bitcoin can change dramatically, but your costs mostly stay the same."

"I was paying about $8,000 per month in electricity," he continued. "When bitcoin was at $20,000, I was making about $14,000 in revenue. Good profit. But at $3,000? My revenue dropped to around $4,000. Suddenly I was losing $4,000 every month."

"Couldn't you just shut down until the price went back up?" Sunil asked.

"Not that simple," Dusan said, shaking his head. "I had contracts for electricity and facility space I still had to pay for. Plus, mining equipment becomes obsolete quickly. If you shut down for a year, your machines might be worthless when you try to restart."

"And I had loans to pay for the equipment," he added. "The banks don't care if Bitcoin crashes. They still want their monthly payment."

They were interrupted by a high pitched beeping coming from one of the monitors. Dusan quickly checked it, typed something, and the beeping stopped.

"Temperature alert," he explained. "One of the cooling units is running hot. Which brings us to the second major risk: hardware failures."

He stood up. "Let me show you."

They walked out to the main floor where rows of ASICs hummed away. The noise level was much higher here, and the air was noticeably warmer despite the cooling systems.

"Each of these machines costs between $5,000 and $15,000," Dusan explained, raising his voice to be heard over the noise. "They run 24/7 at high temperatures. Parts fail regularly."

He pointed to a section where a worker was removing one of the units from a rack. "That one just died this morning. Could be a fan, could be a control board, could be the chips themselves. We'll diagnose it and try to repair it, but sometimes they're just dead."

"How often does that happen?" Sunil asked.

"With proper maintenance, maybe 5% failure rate per year," Dusan replied. "Without good cooling and maintenance? Could be 20% or higher."

"The margins in mining are thin," he continued. "If you lose 20% of your hash power to failures, it can be the difference between profit and loss."

They moved to another area where several disassembled miners were laid out on a workbench. A technician was carefully replacing components on one of them.

"We do most of the repairs in-house now," Dusan said. "Sending them back to manufacturers takes too long and costs too much. But that means we need skilled technicians, spare parts inventory, testing equipment... all additional costs most new miners don't factor in."

"It's like running a ship," Sunil observed. "Always something breaking that needs fixing."

"Exactly," Dusan nodded. "And just like a ship, preventative maintenance is cheaper than emergency repairs."

"Learned that lesson the hard way too?" Sunil asked.

"Oh yeah. In my first operation, I ran the machines as hard as possible with minimal maintenance. Made more money short term, but they died faster and I had more downtime. False economy."

They returned to the office area to escape the noise. On the way, Sunil noticed several security cameras mounted throughout the facility.

"That's another risk," Dusan said, noticing Sunil's gaze. "Security. Both physical and cyber."

Once they were back in the quieter office, Dusan continued, "These machines are valuable and portable. Perfect targets for thieves. We've had attempts. That's why we have cameras, alarm systems, and don't advertise what we do here."

"But physical theft isn't the biggest security risk," he added. "Hacking is."

He turned to one of his monitors. "Mining involves money, lots of it. That attracts hackers. They try to break into pool accounts, mining management systems, even the miners themselves."

"How? I thought Bitcoin was supposed to be secure," Sunil said.

"Bitcoin itself is secure," Dusan explained. "But the systems around it can be vulnerable. If someone hacks the pool you use, they could redirect your earnings to their wallet. Or if they get into your mining management software, they could redirect your hash power to mine for them instead of you."

"It happened to a guy I know," he continued. "He didn't use two factor authentication on his pool account. Hacker got in, changed the pay-out address. He lost two weeks of mining rewards before he noticed."

"Two factor authentication?" Sunil asked.

"When you need your phone to confirm logins," Dusan explained. "Makes it much harder for hackers to get into your accounts, even if they steal your password."

He pulled up another screen showing what looked like monitoring software with various alerts and status indicators. "I track everything. Any unusual changes in hash rate, power consumption, temperature, any login attempts from unknown locations, any changes to pay-out settings. Anything suspicious triggers an alert."

"Seems like a lot to manage," Sunil remarked.

"It is," Dusan agreed. "But it's necessary. Mining is a business with thin margins and significant risks. You need systems to manage those risks."

A beeping sound came from Dusan's phone. He checked it and frowned slightly. "One of my miners at the other facility just went offline. Probably nothing serious, but I'll need to check it when we get back."

"See what I mean?" he said to Sunil. "Always something."

They spent the next hour touring the rest of the facility. Dusan showed him the power distribution systems with backup options, advanced cooling infrastructure, and security setup. Throughout the tour, he shared stories of problems he'd encountered and how he'd solved them.

Eventually, they ended up back in the office area. Dusan brewed fresh coffees and they sat at the small table.

"So what do you think?" Dusan asked. "Scared off yet?"

Sunil thought for a moment. "Not scared, but definitely more aware. There's a lot more that can go wrong than I realized."

"That's the right takeaway," Dusan nodded. "Mining can be profitable, but you need to understand and manage the risks."

"What are the other big risks we haven't covered?" Sunil asked.

"Regulation is a big one," Dusan replied. "Governments can change the rules overnight. China banned mining completely in 2021. Miners there had to shut down or relocate to other countries."

"Could that happen in Europe?"

"Less likely a total ban, but they could impose new taxes, electricity surcharges, or reporting requirements that change the economics." Dusan sipped his coffee. "That's why some larger operations spread out across different countries. Regulatory diversification."

"What about when the difficulty increases? You mentioned that before."

"Good memory," Dusan said. "That's definitely another major risk. If bitcoin's price rises, more miners join the network, difficulty increases, and your share of the rewards decreases. Your costs stay the same, but your revenue drops."

"It's like a treadmill that keeps getting faster," he added. "You have to constantly upgrade your equipment just to stay in place. If you don't, you gradually become less profitable until eventually you're operating at a loss."

Sunil nodded slowly, taking it all in. "So with all these risks, how do you protect yourself? How did you rebuild after losing your first operation?"

"Multiple strategies," Dusan replied. "First, I'm much more conservative with my finances now. I maintain a cash reserve equal to six months of operating expenses. If the market crashes, I can survive the downturn."

"Second, I hedge using Bitcoin futures. If the price drops, my futures position increases in value, offsetting some of the mining revenue loss."

"What are futures?" Sunil asked.

"Financial contracts that let you lock in a future price," Dusan explained. "It's complicated, but basically they let me protect against price drops."

"Third," he continued, "I've diversified my revenue streams. Besides mining Bitcoin directly, I host machines for others and collect fees regardless of bitcoin's price.

"And fourth," he said, "I'm much more disciplined about maintenance and security. Better to spend a little preventing problems than a lot, fixing them."

"The key is thinking like a business owner, not a crypto gambler," he added. "Track your metrics, understand your costs, manage your risks."

He checked one of his monitors and frowned slightly. "Looks like we might have a storm coming in this evening. Better check the backup generator before we head back to the city."

They spent another half hour inspecting the generator and making sure everything was secure in case of power outages. Finally, satisfied that everything was in order, they headed back to Dusan's car.

"That was really helpful," Sunil said as they drove away from the facility. "Not what I expected, but probably what I needed to see."

"Most YouTube videos about mining just show people making money," Dusan nodded. "They don't talk about what happens when things go wrong."

"So is it still worth doing, with all those risks?" Sunil asked.

"It can be, if you go in with open eyes and a solid plan." Dusan turned the car back toward Prague. "Start small, learn the ropes, understand the risks, build up gradually. That's the smart approach."

As they drove back toward the city, Sunil's mind was processing everything he'd seen and heard. Mining was clearly more complex and risky than he'd initially thought, but also more interesting. It wasn't just about setting up machines and watching money roll in. It was a real business with real challenges.

"I've got some contacts in the industry who could help you get started," Dusan said, breaking the silence. "If you decide to try it."

"I think I might," Sunil replied. "But on a smaller scale than I was first thinking. Maybe just one or two machines to learn on."

"That's exactly how I started," Dusan smiled. "One used Antminer in my apartment, keeping my girlfriend awake with the noise. Look where that led."

"To a very understanding ex-girlfriend?" Sunil joked.

"Exactly!" Dusan laughed. "But also to a business I love. Even with all the risks and challenges, there's something satisfying about being part of the Bitcoin network, helping secure the system. Plus, when things go well, the money isn't bad either."

The road stretched ahead of them back toward Prague, the afternoon sun casting long shadows across the landscape. Sunil realized that what had started as simple curiosity about Bitcoin had turned into a potential new direction in his life. One with risks, certainly, but also with possibilities he hadn't considered before.

"So what do you want to see in Prague for your last evening?" Dusan asked as the city skyline came into view in the distance.

"Something that doesn't involve Bitcoin," Sunil replied with a grin. "I think my brain needs a break."

"Fair enough," Dusan laughed. "How about some good Czech food and maybe a jazz club I know? No talk of mining, hashrates, or bitcoin prices allowed."

"Perfect," Sunil agreed. "Though I still have questions about the legal stuff we barely touched on. Like what happens if regulations change?"

Dusan glanced over at him. "That's actually a whole other can of worms. The legal and regulatory landscape for mining is constantly shifting. Every country has different rules, and they change all the time."

"Is that something we should talk about before I decide whether to try mining?" Sunil asked.

"Definitely," Dusan nodded. "Let's grab dinner first, then we can get into the legal side of things. It's not as technical as the hardware stuff, but maybe even more important in the long run."

Sunil nodded, looking forward to experiencing a different side of Prague before digging into yet another aspect of mining. The more he learned, the more he realized how complex this world really was.

CHAPTER 12
LEGAL AND REGULATORY CONSIDERATIONS

The restaurant Dusan picked was hidden on some narrow street you'd walk right past if you didn't know it was there. One of those old places with stone walls that looked like they'd been standing since medieval times. When they walked in, Sunil could smell spices and roasting duck that made his stomach growl after their long day.

"Found this place during my first month in Prague," Dusan said as they squeezed into a small wooden booth. "You never see tourists here."

A waitress brought them menus and two glasses of water with lemon. The lighting was dim, mostly just candles on the tables and a few old lamps hanging from the ceiling beams. In the corner, three musicians were unpacking their instruments.

"So," Sunil said, looking at the menu with dishes he couldn't pronounce, "you were gonna explain all the legal stuff with mining."

"Right," Dusan nodded. "Not nearly as exciting as the hardware, but probably more important if you want to stay in business."

The waitress came back and Dusan ordered for both of them in Czech. "Got us the roast duck with cranberries and bread dumplings," he told Sunil. "It's what they're known for."

"So legal stuff," Sunil prompted once she left.

"Yeah," Dusan took a drink of water. "So here's the deal. Bitcoin mining exists in this weird space where the laws haven't really caught up yet."

"What do you mean?"

"Well, some countries have made mining completely legal with clear rules. Others have banned it outright. But most places are somewhere in between, with old laws that weren't written with Bitcoin in mind."

Dusan grabbed a roll from the basket on the table. "Like here in the Czech Republic. No law specifically says 'Bitcoin mining is legal.' But it's not illegal either. We just operate under normal business laws and tax codes that weren't designed for mining."

"And that's a problem?"

"The biggest issue is uncertainty. The rules could change tomorrow, and suddenly your whole operation is illegal or just not profitable anymore."

Their food arrived, steaming plates with crispy duck, red cranberry sauce, and fluffy white dumplings on the side. Sunil took a bite and his eyes widened. The duck was perfectly tender with crispy skin.

"Good, right?" Dusan grinned, seeing his reaction. "Anyway, the legal stuff basically breaks down into three main areas: taxes, environmental regulations, and local permits."

"Let's start with taxes," Sunil said, cutting another piece of duck.

"Usually the first headache," Dusan nodded. "In most countries, when you mine Bitcoin, that's taxable income right when you receive it."

"How does that work exactly?"

"Say you mine 0.1 bitcoin today, and bitcoin is worth $50,000. According to most tax authorities, you just made $5,000 in taxable income. You got to report that and pay tax on it."

"Even though you didn't sell it for actual money?" Sunil frowned.

"Exactly. And then later, if bitcoin goes up to $60,000 and you sell, you pay capital gains tax on that $1,000 increase."

"So you get taxed twice? That seems unfair."

"Yeah, it's not great," Dusan said, swallowing a bite of dumpling. "But some countries are different. Some only tax when you convert to fiat money. The rules are all over the place."

"How do you keep track of all that?"

"I have an accountant who specializes in crypto. Not cheap, but worth every penny," Dusan said. "The worst part is even most tax professionals don't know the right answers. The rules aren't clear."

The jazz trio started playing quietly, a slow melody that somehow matched the centuries old restaurant and the warm food.

"What about reporting?" Sunil asked. "Do you have to tell the government every single Bitcoin you mine?"

"Generally yeah," Dusan said, pulling out his phone. "Look, I use this app to track everything. When I mined it, how much, what it was worth that day. If I get audited, I need these records."

"Seems like a lot of work."

"It is. Some miners try to skip it, but that's asking for trouble. Tax authorities are getting better at tracking crypto transactions. Better to just follow the rules, even when they're not totally clear."

They ate quietly for a minute, the only sounds were the soft jazz and the clink of knives and forks on plates.

"I've read articles claiming Bitcoin mining is terrible for the environment," Sunil said eventually. "Is that true?"

Dusan rolled his eyes. "It's more complicated than those articles make it sound. There are legitimate environmental concerns and regulations you need to deal with."

"Like what?"

"Energy consumption is the big one. Some areas have special taxes on high energy users, or won't let you use full power during peak times."

He wiped his mouth with a napkin before continuing. "Then there's noise. You heard how loud those miners are today. If you set up near houses, you might break noise ordinances."

"What else?"

"Heat discharge is another issue," Dusan continued. "Some places regulate how much heat you can put into the air or water systems if you're using water cooling."

"There are that many regulations specifically for mining?" Sunil looked surprised.

"Not specifically for mining, no. These are general environmental regulations that affect mining operations because of how much power we use, how noisy the machines are, and how much heat they generate." Dusan pointed to Sunil's plate. "Try the dumplings with the cranberry sauce. It's incredible."

Sunil tried the combination and nodded appreciatively. "So how do you deal with all these environmental rules?"

"Several ways," Dusan replied. "First, location is key. I picked spots away from residential areas, with good access to renewable energy when possible."

"Second, I invest in efficiency. Better cooling systems, more efficient miners, heat recycling when possible. It's better for the environment and saves money too."

"And third, I stay informed about changing regulations. Some places are creating mining specific rules, especially around power consumption. You need to watch out for those and adapt before they become law."

The waitress cleared their empty plates and asked if they wanted dessert. They both ordered apple strudel and hot tea.

"What about local regulations?" Sunil asked once she'd left. "Like zoning and stuff?"

"That can be the trickiest part," Dusan nodded. "Most cities never imagined they'd need rules for cryptocurrency mining. So you end up dealing with a bunch of different permits and regulations."

"Such as?"

"Building permits, for one. Converting a space for mining usually requires electrical upgrades, ventilation systems, maybe structural changes. All of that needs permits."

"Then there's zoning," he continued. "Is mining considered industrial? Commercial? Data processing? Different cities classify it differently, which affects where you can set up."

"And don't forget business licenses," Dusan added. "Some places now require special licenses for crypto businesses."

Their dessert and tea arrived, warm strudel with cinnamon and vanilla sauce on the side.

"How do you keep track of all this stuff?" Sunil asked, taking a bite of the flaky pastry. "It sounds like a nightmare."

"I have a lawyer who specializes in this area," Dusan admitted. "Again, not cheap, but worth it. He keeps me updated on changing regulations, helps with compliance and deals with authorities when needed."

"Is that necessary for a small operation? If I just had a few miners to start?"

"Maybe not at first," Dusan conceded. "If you're just running a couple machines at home, you might fly under the radar. But as soon as you start scaling up, get proper legal advice. The fines for breaking the rules can be huge."

The jazz music picked up tempo slightly, and more customers filled the small restaurant. The atmosphere was warm and lively.

"Any other legal issues I should know about?" Sunil asked, finishing his strudel.

"Electricity contracts are important," Dusan replied. "Many residential power agreements don't allow commercial usage or have limits on consumption. If you suddenly start pulling massive power for mining, your utility company might investigate or even cut you off."

He sipped his tea. "And insurance is another thing to think about. Normal policies usually don't cover cryptocurrency equipment or losses. You need specialized coverage."

"Sounds like a lot to deal with," Sunil said, looking slightly overwhelmed.

"It is," Dusan nodded. "But here's the thing. Understanding the legal landscape isn't just about avoiding problems. It's also about finding opportunities."

"How so?"

"Some places are actively trying to attract Bitcoin miners. They offer tax breaks, easier permitting, sometimes even cheaper electricity." Dusan leaned forward. "Texas, Wyoming, and parts of Northern Europe are competing for mining operations. If you know where to look, the regulations can actually work in your favour."

"So it's not all bad news?"

"Not at all," Dusan smiled. "It's just part of the business. Every industry has rules to follow."

They finished their tea, and Dusan paid the bill despite Sunil's attempts to split it.

"My treat," he insisted. "Consider it part of your mining education."

They stepped outside into the cool evening air. The streets of Old Town were lit with warm yellow lamps, and people wandered along the cobblestones, popping into shops and restaurants.

"We still have time before the jazz club starts," Dusan said, checking his watch. "Want to walk around a bit?"

They strolled through the narrow streets, past buildings that had stood for centuries and small squares with fountains. Prague at night had a magical feeling, the old architecture lit up against the dark sky.

"So with all these legal hoops to jump through," Sunil said as they walked, "how did you actually get your mining business off the ground? Where did you even start?"

Dusan smiled. "That's a whole other conversation. Building a mining business from scratch is quite a journey. I made a ton of mistakes along the way."

"Like what?"

"Like not having a proper business plan. Not understanding market cycles. Expanding too quickly before I knew what I was doing." Dusan shook his head. "Looking back, I'm amazed my business survived those early years."

"But you learned from it?"

"For sure. Now I have systems for everything, proper financing, business structure and growth strategy." He glanced at Sunil. "That might be the most valuable thing I could share with you. How to build a sustainable mining business, not just a hobby operation."

"I'd like to hear about that," Sunil nodded. "If I'm going to try this, I want to do it right from the start."

"Smart," Dusan approved. "Let's check out the jazz club, and I can walk you through how to approach building a real mining business. Not just buying some equipment and hoping for the best, but creating something that can survive market crashes and grow over time."

They turned a corner and could hear music coming from a basement venue ahead. The sign above the door simply read "Jazz."

"Sounds good to me," Sunil said. "I've got plenty more questions about the business side of things."

As they headed down the steps into the club, Sunil realized how quickly he'd been drawn into this world. What had started as casual curiosity had turned into serious consideration of a mining business. If he was going to do this, he wanted to understand not just the technology and risks, but how to build something that would last. And it seemed Dusan had plenty more wisdom to share on exactly that topic.

CHAPTER 13 BUILDING A BITCOIN MINING BUSINESS

The jazz club was in a basement down a narrow set of stairs. The ceiling was low with exposed pipes painted black, and the walls were covered with old album covers and posters of jazz greats. A small stage in the corner held a quartet playing something smooth and mellow. The place was about half full, mostly locals by the looks of it.

"Nice spot," Sunil said as they found a small table toward the back where they could still talk.

"Been coming here for years," Dusan replied. "The owner is a friend. They do live music every night."

A waitress in all black came over, and they both ordered mint tea. The music was loud enough to feel but not so loud they couldn't hear each other.

"So," Sunil said once the waitress left, "you were going to tell me about building an actual mining business. Not just running a few machines."

"Right," Dusan nodded. "This is where most miners fail, honestly. They focus so much on the tech that they forget it's a business."

"What do you mean?"

"Well, think about it. Anyone can buy some ASICs and plug them in. But that doesn't make it a sustainable business. You need a real business model."

Their teas arrived, steaming and fragrant. Dusan thanked the waitress in Czech.

"So what are the common business models?" Sunil asked, dropping a sugar cube into his cup.

"There are several," Dusan said, stirring his own tea. "The simplest is just mining Bitcoin yourself and holding or selling it. That's how most people start, including me."

"But there are other approaches," he continued. "Hosting is a big one. That's where you provide space, power, and maintenance for other people's mining equipment. You charge a monthly fee regardless of bitcoin's price."

"Like renting out space in your facility?" Sunil asked.

"Exactly. It gives you steady income even when Bitcoin crashes. Plus your customers take on the market risk while you make money either way."

The jazz band finished their song, and the small crowd applauded. They started a new number, something with a faster beat.

"What other models are there?" Sunil asked.

"Cloud mining is popular but risky," Dusan replied. "That's where you sell mining contracts to people who don't want to deal with hardware at all. They pay you, and you give them a share of mining rewards."

"Sounds easy."

"For the customers, yeah. But for the provider, it's tricky. You're promising future returns in a volatile market. Lots of cloud mining companies have gone bust because they promised more than they could deliver."

Dusan blew on his tea to cool it. "Then there's the service model. Mining consultation, facility design, maintenance contracts. That's actually a growing part of my business now."

"Is that what you'd recommend for someone starting out?" Sunil asked.

"No, not at first," Dusan shook his head. "Start with your own operation. Learn the ropes. Build a track record. Then you can expand into services once you know what you're doing."

A server walked by with a plate of small desserts, and Dusan flagged him down. "The honey cake here is amazing," he told Sunil as he ordered two slices.

"So let's say I start small and want to grow," Sunil said. "How do you fund something like that? Those machines aren't cheap."

"That's the million dollar question," Dusan laughed. "Literally. Raising capital is one of the biggest challenges."

"What options are there?"

"Well, the bootstrap approach is how most start. Use your own savings to buy a few machines, reinvest the profits to buy more. That's how I began."

"Slow but safe," Sunil nodded.

"Exactly. The benefit is you don't owe anyone anything. The downside is slow growth. It took me three years to build up to fifty machines that way."

The honey cake arrived, two generous slices with cream on top. Sunil took a bite and raised his eyebrows in pleasant surprise.

"Good, right?" Dusan grinned. "Anyway, beyond bootstrapping, there are several funding approaches. Traditional bank loans are tough to get for mining, though. Banks don't understand the business well enough yet."

"What about investors?" Sunil asked.

"That's more common," Dusan nodded. "Angel investors, small venture capital firms, sometimes family offices. They typically want equity in your business in exchange for capital."

"How do you even find those people?"

"Networking, mostly. Crypto conferences, mining events, online communities. I met my first investor at a Bitcoin meetup right here in Prague."

Dusan took another bite of cake before continuing. "Equipment financing is another option. Some manufacturers or distributors will finance the ASICs directly. You make monthly payments plus interest."

"Like a car loan but for mining rigs?"

"Pretty much. The machines themselves are the collateral. If you default, they take them back."

The jazz music shifted to a slower, more contemplative piece. The lights dimmed slightly, creating an even more intimate atmosphere.

"What about mining pools? Do they offer funding?" Sunil asked.

"Some are starting to," Dusan replied. "There are pools that will front you the money for equipment in exchange for a commitment to mine with them for a certain period. Not a bad arrangement if the terms are fair."

Sunil finished his cake and sat back. "So let's say I've figured out funding. How do you actually scale from a few machines to a real business?"

"That's where most people mess up," Dusan said. "They think scaling is just buying more of the same machines. But real scaling requires systems and processes."

"Like what?"

"Like monitoring software that can handle hundreds of machines, not just a few. Maintenance protocols. Spare parts inventory. Staff training. Heat management solutions that work at scale."

Dusan counted on his fingers. "You need proper accounting systems. Legal structures. Banking relationships. Insurance. It's a whole different game from running a few miners in your garage."

"Did you figure all that out yourself?" Sunil asked.

"Hell no," Dusan laughed. "Made tons of mistakes. Lost a lot of money in the process. Eventually I had to bring in a consultant who specialises in mining operations to help me sort everything out properly. Best decision I ever made, honestly."

"That's why I say start small, learn, then scale gradually. And don't be afraid to get professional help when you need it."

A couple at a nearby table got up to dance near the band, swaying slowly to the music. The club had filled up more as they talked, creating a lively but still comfortable atmosphere.

"What about marketing?" Sunil asked after a moment. "Do you need to advertise a mining business?"

"Depends on your model," Dusan replied. "If you're just mining Bitcoin yourself, not really. The network doesn't care who you are."

"But if you're offering hosting or services, then yes, marketing becomes important. Though it's not traditional marketing like you might think."

"What do you mean?"

"It's very relationship driven," Dusan explained. "Most of my hosting clients came through word of mouth. Someone knows someone who needs mining space. Or they met me at a conference. Traditional advertising doesn't work as well in this industry."

"So networking is the main thing?"

"Absolutely. Being active in mining communities, speaking at events, sharing knowledge on forums or Twitter. Building a reputation as someone who knows their stuff and can be trusted."

Dusan checked his watch. "The band's about to take a break. Want to order something else?"

They both got another tea, and Dusan continued his explanation.

"One marketing approach that works well is content. Technical guides, market analysis, facility tours on YouTube. Establishing yourself as an expert."

"Kind of like what you're doing with me right now," Sunil observed with a smile.

"Exactly," Dusan grinned. "Though you're getting the friend rate. I usually charge for this kind of consultation."

"You mean people pay you just for mining advice?"

"More and more, actually," Dusan nodded. "As my reputation has grown, I get companies or wealthy individuals asking for help setting up their operations. They'd rather pay someone with experience than make expensive mistakes."

"That sounds like a pretty good gig," Sunil remarked.

"It is," Dusan agreed. "Lower risk than running my own mining farm, though I still do both. Consulting lets me leverage my knowledge without all the capital investment and market risk."

The band returned from their break and started playing again, this time something more upbeat that had several couples moving to the dance floor.

"I never would have thought of mining as something you could consult on," Sunil said. "But I guess it makes sense with how complex it is."

"It's becoming a whole industry within the industry," Dusan said. "Site selection consultants. Power contract negotiators. ASIC procurement specialists. Cooling system designers. There are people who just focus on one aspect of mining and make a good living advising others."

"Is that something you'd recommend? Becoming a consultant?"

"Not right away," Dusan shook his head. "You need real experience first. Nobody's going to pay for your advice until you've proven you can do it successfully yourself."

"But down the road, it's definitely worth considering. Especially if you develop expertise in a specific niche."

Sunil nodded thoughtfully, sipping his tea. "This has been really helpful. Gives me a much clearer picture of how to approach this if I decide to try it."

"Speaking of that," Dusan said, "have you thought about what kind of mining operation would make sense for you, given your sailing schedule?"

"I'm still figuring that out," Sunil admitted. "Obviously I couldn't run something that needs daily attention while I'm at sea."

"You know," Dusan said, leaning forward slightly, "there might be an interesting middle path for someone like you. You could start small, learn the ropes, build some expertise, and then leverage that knowledge while still keeping your sailing career."

"How so?"

"Well, you travel all over, right? Meet all kinds of people? That's perfect for building an international network. And you probably have more technical knowledge than most, just from working on ships."

"I guess that's true," Sunil nodded.

"You could position yourself as someone who understands both worlds," Dusan continued, warming to the idea. "Maritime industry and Bitcoin mining. Maybe even focus on helping shipping companies optimize their energy usage with Bitcoin mining. There's a growing trend of using excess energy from industrial operations for mining."

"That's actually... not a bad idea," Sunil said slowly. "I do know the shipping industry inside out."

"That's the thing about consulting," Dusan smiled. "It's all about finding your unique angle. But first, you need to understand mining from the inside. No shortcuts there."

"How would I even start down that path?" Sunil asked.

"That's a whole other conversation," Dusan replied, finishing his tea. "And it's getting late. But we've got plenty of time to cover that. How long can you stay in Prague?"

"Well, I was supposed to fly out tomorrow night," Sunil said, then paused. "But honestly, this mining stuff is way more interesting than being a regular tourist. I think I'm going to rebook my flight and stay a few more days."

"Perfect," Dusan nodded. "We can spend the next few days diving deeper. I can even introduce you to some people in the industry here in Prague if you want."

"That would be awesome," Sunil said. "I'm all in at this point. Might as well learn as much as I can while I'm here."

"Great," Dusan grinned. "Tomorrow I can show you how I built my consulting side of the business. It's actually become almost as profitable as the mining itself, with a lot less headache."

"Definitely interested," Sunil nodded.

As the jazz played on and the night grew later, Sunil found himself mentally sketching out possibilities. The idea of combining his maritime knowledge with this new world of Bitcoin mining was intriguing. Maybe there was a way to have a foot in both worlds after all.

CHAPTER 14
CONSULTANCY IN BITCOIN MINING

Sunil woke up to his phone buzzing. It was almost 11 AM, way later than he usually slept. The jazz club had gone on until the early hours, and by the time they'd made it back to their hotel, the sky was already getting light.

He grabbed his phone. A text from Dusan: "Meet at Cafe Louvre at noon. Perfect place to discuss consulting. Been there since 1902. Einstein used to hang out there."

After a quick shower, Sunil headed out. The cafe wasn't far from his hotel, and the morning was bright and clear, perfect for walking through Prague's winding streets. He found the place easily enough, an elegant cafe on the second floor of a grand old building. Inside was all high ceilings, marble tables, and dark wood panelling. The kind of place where you could imagine philosophers and scientists debating big ideas a century ago.

Dusan was already there, sitting at a corner table with coffee and a small plate of pastries in front of him.

"This place is something else," Sunil said, sliding into the chair across from him.

"One of the oldest cafes in Europe," Dusan nodded. "I thought it was fitting to talk about consulting here. This is where deals get made in Prague."

Indeed, looking around, Sunil noticed several tables with people in business attire, papers spread out between them, talking in hushed tones.

"So, mining consultant," Sunil said after ordering a coffee from a passing waiter. "How does someone get into that?"

"Usually by accident," Dusan laughed. "That's how it happened for me. I was running my own operation, and people kept asking me for advice. Eventually I realized I could charge for what I was giving away for free."

"Is there actually that much demand?" Sunil asked, helping himself to one of the pastries.

"Way more than you'd think," Dusan replied. "Think about it. Bitcoin mining has huge potential rewards but also enormous risks. People with money want to get in, but they don't want to make expensive mistakes. They'll pay good money for someone who can help them avoid those mistakes."

"So what kind of consulting do you actually do?"

"Couple different types," Dusan said, sipping his coffee. "First is strategic consulting. That's helping clients figure out if mining makes sense for them at all, what scale to start at, what business model to use, how to structure their operation."

"Then there's technical consulting. Hardware selection, facility design, cooling systems, power management, software setup. The nuts and bolts of making a mining operation work efficiently."

The waiter brought Sunil's coffee, and he took a grateful sip. He was still feeling the effects of the late night.

"Who are your typical clients?" he asked.

"All over the map," Dusan replied. "I've worked with wealthy individuals who want to diversify into Bitcoin. Small business owners looking to start mining on the side. Even some institutional investors, testing the waters."

"But my favourite clients are industrial operations with excess energy. Factories, power plants, oil and gas companies. They have power that's going to waste, and mining is a perfect way to monetize it."

"How do you even find these clients?" Sunil asked.

"At first you don't, they find you," Dusan said. "You need to build a reputation first. That's the foundation of consulting success."

"How'd you build yours?"

"Several ways," Dusan counted on his fingers. "I started sharing knowledge on forums and Reddit. Answering questions, posting guides, helping newbies troubleshoot. Built a name for myself as someone who knows their stuff."

"Then I started speaking at small Bitcoin meetups, then bigger conferences. Wrote some articles for Bitcoin publications. Created case studies of my own mining operations, sharing real numbers and lessons learned."

He gestured around the cafe. "And a lot of networking. Mining is still small enough that reputation travels fast. Do good work for one client, and they'll refer three more."

A group at a nearby table burst into laughter, momentarily drawing their attention. They looked like tourists, probably Americans by their accents, enjoying the historic atmosphere.

"What about credentials?" Sunil asked, turning back to Dusan. "Do you need certifications or something?"

"Not really," Dusan shook his head. "There are no official mining consultant certifications. What matters is demonstrable experience and results. My portfolio *IS* my credential."

"Portfolio?"

"Documentation of projects I've worked on," Dusan explained. "Before and after metrics for operations I've optimized. Facility designs I've created. Power savings achieved. ROI improvements. All with client permission, of course."

"Speaking of clients," Sunil said, "what are the legal aspects of consulting? Contracts and stuff?"

"That's super important," Dusan nodded seriously. "When I started, I was just helping people informally. Big mistake. You need proper contracts to protect yourself."

He pulled out his phone and showed Sunil a document. "This is my standard consulting agreement template. Has all the legal protections: scope of work, deliverables, payment terms, confidentiality, liability limitations."

"Liability limitations?"

"Crucial," Dusan emphasized. "Mining is inherently risky. Markets crash, equipment fails, regulations change. Your contract needs to make clear that you're providing advice, not guarantees. Otherwise, you could get sued when things go wrong."

"Has that happened to you?" Sunil asked.

"Not to me personally, but I know consultants who've been sued by clients who lost money mining. That's why I'm careful about setting realistic expectations and documenting everything."

The waiter came by to refill their coffees. The cafe had gotten busier, with most tables now occupied. Through the tall windows, Sunil could see people strolling along the street below, enjoying the nice weather.

"What about ethics?" Sunil asked after the waiter left. "Are there lines you won't cross?"

"Absolutely," Dusan said firmly. "I never recommend mining if I don't think it makes financial sense for the client. I've turned down good money because I knew their plan wouldn't work."

"I also won't help with anything legally questionable. No power theft schemes, no tax evasion strategies, no mining in jurisdictions where it's banned."

"Do people actually ask for that stuff?" Sunil looked surprised.

"More often than you'd think," Dusan grimaced. "Especially when bitcoin prices are high and everyone's trying to get in quick. Part of being a good consultant is knowing when to say no."

He finished his coffee and signalled for the check. "Let's walk a bit. I've been sitting too long."

They paid and headed out into the sunshine. The street was lined with shops and cafes, with the spires of Prague Castle visible in the distance.

"So how do you price your services?" Sunil asked as they walked. "That seems tricky with something like mining consulting."

"I use different models depending on the project," Dusan replied. "For simple advisory sessions, just helping someone decide if mining is right for them, I charge an hourly rate."

"For bigger projects, like designing a mining facility, I'll do a flat project fee with clear deliverables. And for ongoing optimization and management consulting, sometimes I do a monthly retainer."

"What about success fees?" Sunil asked. "Like getting a percentage of profits?"

"I avoid those now," Dusan shook his head. "Tried it early on, but it gets messy. Too many variables outside your control affect mining profitability. I prefer clean, straightforward compensation."

They turned down a narrower street, quieter than the main thoroughfare. Dusan paused to look in the window of a small bookshop.

"The most important thing about pricing," he continued, "is understanding the value you provide. I don't charge based on my time, but on how much money I can save or make for the client."

"Like what?"

"Well, if my facility design saves a client $50,000 in cooling costs, or my strategy increases their mining efficiency by 20%, that's worth a lot more than just my hours."

"Makes sense," Sunil nodded. "So what makes someone a really good mining consultant? Besides technical knowledge."

"The ability to create custom strategies," Dusan said without hesitation. "Cookie cutter approaches don't work in mining because every client has different circumstances."

"For example?" Sunil prompted.

"Say I have two clients. Both want to start mining, both have similar budgets. But one has access to cheap hydroelectric power in a cold climate. The other has higher electricity costs but owns a building with extra space."

Dusan paused as they waited to cross a street. "They need completely different strategies. The first might focus on maximizing hash rate, running equipment at full power because electricity is cheap. The second might focus on efficiency, using the latest ASICs that give the most hash per watt, maybe even underclocking to reduce power consumption."

"That's the art of consulting," he continued as they crossed. "Taking all the variables, the client's resources, risk tolerance, goals, and location, and crafting a strategy that makes sense for their specific situation."

They walked a while longer, Dusan pointing out interesting buildings and sharing bits of Prague history. Eventually, they found themselves in a small square with a fountain in the centre. The area was less touristy, with locals going about their day.

"You know," Dusan said, sitting on a bench near the fountain, "there's a natural progression from miner to consultant, but you need to be good at both the technical and business sides."

"How so?" Sunil asked, joining him on the bench.

"Well, clients don't just want someone who can tell them what equipment to buy. They want someone who understands the whole picture. Market trends, regulatory risks, power contracts, cooling technology, operational efficiency."

He watched a group of children playing by the fountain. "And you need to be good at explaining complex things simply. Mining is technical, but your clients often aren't technical people. They're investors, business owners, executives."

"Seems like you need to be both technical and a people person," Sunil observed.

"Exactly," Dusan nodded. "Technical knowledge gets you in the door, but communication skills make you effective. And problem solving ability keeps clients coming back."

"Problem solving?"

"Mining operations always have issues," Dusan explained. "Machines fail, cooling systems underperform, hash rates drop. A good consultant doesn't just design systems, they troubleshoot them when things go wrong."

"Actually," he continued, checking his phone, "I'm meeting a client tomorrow who's having efficiency problems at their facility. You should come along. Good chance to see the troubleshooting and optimization side of consulting in action."

"I'd like that," Sunil nodded. "Seeing the theory put into practice."

"It's usually the most interesting part," Dusan said, standing up. "Figuring out why an operation isn't performing as expected and fixing it. Sometimes it's obvious, sometimes it's like detective work."

As they continued their walk through Prague, Sunil found himself thinking more seriously about the consulting path. The idea of helping others navigate the complex world of mining, drawing on his technical knowledge from ships combined with what he was learning about Bitcoin, was appealing. And the fact that it could be done remotely, even while still working on ships part of the year, made it seem like a realistic possibility.

"Got time for lunch?" Dusan asked, interrupting his thoughts. "There's a great place nearby, and I can tell you more about how I structure my client engagements."

"Definitely," Sunil replied. The day was still young, and there was much more to learn about this unexpected career path that seemed to combine technical expertise, business acumen, and helping others avoid costly mistakes.

CHAPTER 15
TROUBLESHOOTING AND OPTIMIZING MINING OPERATIONS

After lunch, Dusan checked his watch. "Got some time before the meetup. Want to see something cool? My buddy Viktor lets me use his place as a workshop while I'm in Prague. It's where I do all my testing and fixing."

Viktor's apartment was in a neighbourhood called Vinohrady, about twenty minutes by tram from the restaurant. It was in an old, fancy building with ornate stonework around the windows and a heavy wooden door at the entrance.

"Fourth floor," Dusan said as they entered. "No elevator, sorry."

When they reached the apartment, Sunil was surprised by what he saw inside. The living room had been converted into what looked like a mini mining operation and workshop. Several mining rigs hummed away on metal shelves, while a workbench covered in tools and parts took up one wall. Three monitors displayed various charts and data streams.

"Welcome to the Prague lab," Dusan said, seeing Sunil's expression. "Viktor's an old mining buddy. He travels a lot for work, so he lets me use his place when I'm in town. Perfect for testing and troubleshooting."

"You run all this in Viktor's apartment?" Sunil asked, feeling the warmth in the room from the operating machines.

"Just a few test units," Dusan replied. "My main operation is outside Prague. These are for trying new setups and fixing problems when I'm in the city."

He pointed to a machine that was partially disassembled on the workbench. "Perfect example right here. This S19 was running at about 60% of expected hash rate. Want to see how I diagnose something like that?"

"Definitely," Sunil said, pulling up a stool next to the workbench.

"First rule of mining troubleshooting," Dusan began, picking up a tablet with charts displayed, "same symptom can have multiple causes. Hash rate drops could be from overheating, power problems, network issues, or hardware failure."

"So how do you figure out which one it is?" Sunil asked.

"Process of elimination, starting with the most common issues," Dusan said, turning to the machine. "In my experience, about 70% of problems are cooling related."

He picked up a handheld device with a digital readout. "Thermal sensor. Let's check the temperatures first."

He pointed the device at various parts of the open miner, reading off numbers. "These chips should run between 60 and 75 degrees Celsius. I'm seeing some at 85, almost 90. That's definitely a problem."

"Is that why the hash rate dropped?"

"Yep. When chips get too hot, they throttle performance to prevent damage," Dusan explained. "But we need to figure out WHY they're overheating."

He grabbed a small flashlight and shined it into the miner. "Look at this. See the fans?"

Sunil leaned in to see that the cooling fans were clogged with dust and barely moving.

"Super common problem," Dusan said. "Dust build-up on the fans. They can't move enough air, so everything overheats." He reached for a can of compressed air. "Simple fix, but you'd be amazed how many miners lose money because they skip basic maintenance."

He thoroughly blew out the fans and heat sinks, sending clouds of dust into the air. Sunil backed up, trying not to breathe it in.

"Sorry," Dusan grinned. "Should have warned you. Mining dust is nasty stuff."

After reassembling the miner and powering it back up, Dusan turned to his monitors. "Now we wait a bit and see if the hash rate recovers. Want something to drink? I've got water, juice, coffee."

They moved to the small kitchen connected to the living room. Dusan grabbed two sodas from the fridge and handed one to Sunil.

"So dust is a common problem. What else?" Sunil asked.

"Power issues are next most common," Dusan said, leaning against the counter. "Inconsistent voltage, failing power supplies, bad connections. I had one client losing thousands a month because their building had old wiring that couldn't handle the load."

"How do you diagnose power problems?"

"Multi-meter is your best friend," Dusan replied. "Check the voltage coming into the miners, check the output from the power supplies. Look for fluctuations or drops under load."

He took a sip of his soda. "Then there's software and firmware issues. Outdated firmware, configuration errors, software conflicts."

"How often do you update firmware?" Sunil asked.

"Depends. Manufacturer updates might come every few months, but I don't always install them right away," Dusan said. "I test new firmware on one machine first to make sure it doesn't cause problems. Never update all your miners at once."

They returned to the living room where Dusan checked the miner they'd cleaned. "Look at that," he said, pointing to a chart on one of the screens. "Hash rate is already up 20% and still climbing. Sometimes the simplest fix makes the biggest difference."

"What about hardware failures?" Sunil asked. "Things that can't be fixed with cleaning or updates?"

"They happen," Dusan nodded. "Control boards go bad, chips fail, connectors corrode. Here, let me show you something."

He moved to another miner that was open on the workbench and pointed to a row of small components. "See these capacitors? They're slightly bulging at the top. That's a sign they're failing. Left unfixed, they'll eventually blow and take the whole board with them."

"Can you replace just those parts?"

"If you've got the skills," Dusan said. "I do component level repair for some things, but it requires soldering equipment and steady hands. Most miners just replace the entire board, which is more expensive but faster."

He walked over to a cabinet and opened it to reveal shelves of organized parts. "This is essential for serious mining. Spare parts inventory. Fans, power supplies, control boards, cables. When something fails, you want replacement parts on hand. Waiting for shipping can cost days of mining time."

"Seems like a lot to learn," Sunil remarked.

"You pick it up as you go," Dusan assured him. "Start with one machine, learn its quirks, then expand. That's how I did it."

He sat down at his desk and pulled up what looked like a spreadsheet. "This is another critical part of mining: documentation. I log every problem, solution, and upgrade. Date, symptoms, what fixed it, parts used, time spent."

"Why so detailed?"

"Patterns," Dusan explained. "Over time, you start seeing which machines have which problems. Maybe one model always has fan issues at the six month mark. Another has power supply failures. That helps you do preventative maintenance before things break."

Sunil nodded. "Like changing the oil in a car before the engine has problems."

"Exactly! Preventative maintenance is always cheaper than emergency repairs."

Dusan switched to another screen showing graphs of various miners' performance. "This brings us to upgrading for better performance. Sometimes it's not about fixing problems but improving what already works."

"Like overclocking?" Sunil asked, remembering their conversation from earlier.

"That's one way, yeah. But there are less risky upgrades too. Better cooling solutions, firmware optimizations, more efficient power supplies."

He pointed to a row of miners that looked slightly different from the others. "These I've modified with improved heat sinks and better fans. About 15% more efficient with minimal risk."

He clicked through several more screens of data. "This is what I wanted to show you most. Monitoring tools are absolutely essential for successful mining."

The screen showed dashboards with real time data on dozens of miners, their hash rates, temperatures, power consumption, and more.

"For home setups, something simple like Awesome Miner or basic monitoring tools work fine," Dusan explained. "They'll alert you if a miner goes offline or the hash rate drops."

"But once you start scaling up, you need something more robust. That's where HiveOS really shines," he continued, navigating to another screen. "It's honestly one of the best monitoring tools currently in the market."

"What makes it special?" Sunil asked, leaning closer to look at the interface.

"Several things," Dusan said, pointing at different sections of the dashboard. "First, the troubleshooting features are incredible. If a miner starts acting up, HiveOS can automatically diagnose what's wrong. Overheating? It'll tell you which specific chip. Hash rate dropping? It identifies exactly which hashboard is having issues."

"Plus, it has remote management capabilities," he added. "I can restart miners, change pool settings, even update firmware from anywhere in the world. No need to physically visit the mining site."

He pulled out his phone and showed Sunil an app. "For even larger operations, you can layer additional monitoring on top. This sends me alerts 24/7 for any issues. Temperature spikes, hash rate changes, power consumption fluctuations, network problems, everything."

"You get a lot of alerts?" Sunil asked.

"At least a few every day across all my miners," Dusan nodded. "Most are minor, but catching problems early prevents bigger issues later. HiveOS catches most problems before they become serious, but having multiple layers of monitoring gives me complete peace of mind."

He scrolled through the app, showing various alerts and reports. "The reporting side is just as important as monitoring. Weekly efficiency reports, profitability per machine, power usage trends. Data helps you make better decisions about when to upgrade, repair, or retire equipment."

Sunil watched as Dusan navigated through complex screens of information with ease. It was clear he'd spent years developing these systems.

"For someone just starting out, what's the minimum monitoring setup you'd recommend?" Sunil asked.

"At minimum, you want alerts for offline machines, temperature thresholds, and significant hash rate drops," Dusan replied. "And keep daily records of overall performance and any issues. Even a simple spreadsheet is better than nothing."

He checked the time on his phone. "We should head out soon if we want to make it to that meetup I mentioned. There's a monthly gathering of miners at a cafe not far from here."

"Just one more question," Sunil said. "Of all the problems you've encountered, what was the strangest or most difficult to solve?"

Dusan laughed. "Oh man, I've seen some weird ones. Had a client whose hash rate would drop every day between 2 and 4 PM. Turned out their facility was next to a school, and when all the kids got online after classes, it congested the local internet infrastructure."

"How'd you fix that?"

"Had to set up a dedicated connection that bypassed the local ISP," Dusan said. "But that's the thing about mining problems. They're rarely just technical issues. They're often about the environment, infrastructure, or how systems interact."

He started shutting down the workstation. "You know what might help you more than all this technical talk? Some real-world case studies of successful mining operations. The theory is important, but seeing how people actually built profitable setups from scratch is even better."

"That would be really helpful," Sunil nodded. "Concrete examples of what works."

"I've got some great ones," Dusan said, gathering his things. "Stories of miners who started small and scaled up smartly. Shows the different approaches people take based on their unique situations."

"They'll be there today?" Sunil asked.

"Should be," Dusan said, grabbing a jacket. "They've got some great stories about building their operations. One started in his garage and now runs a facility with thousands of machines. Another found a niche mining in extreme cold environments where nobody else wanted to operate."

"I'd like to hear about that," Sunil said. "Seems like there are a lot of different paths to success."

"That's the thing about Bitcoin mining," Dusan said as they headed for the door. "There's no single right way to do it. These guys all took different approaches based on their unique situations and resources. But there are common principles they all followed."

As they left the apartment and headed down the stairs, Sunil found himself increasingly drawn to the problem-solving aspects of mining. The technical challenges reminded him of troubleshooting ship systems, but with the added complexity of market forces and constant technological evolution.

The afternoon sun was warm as they stepped outside, the streets of Prague filled with people enjoying the pleasant weather. Sunil was eager to hear more about these real-world mining operations Dusan had mentioned. There was something compelling about actual case studies that even the best theoretical knowledge couldn't match.

CHAPTER 16
CASE STUDIES AND SUCCESS STORIES

The meetup spot turned out to be this old warehouse they'd fixed up as some kind of tech hangout. Not what Sunil expected. Inside was all brick walls and wooden tables, with people clustered in groups, some typing away on laptops, others just talking.

"Not bad, huh?" Dusan said as they grabbed coffees from a counter in the back. "Used to be a factory or something."

They found a couple chairs in a corner away from the noisier groups. The evening sun was coming through these huge windows, making dust particles visible in the air.

"Before we dive into stories, let me introduce you to some people," Dusan said, scanning the room. "Ah, perfect timing."

He waved over two men who were chatting near the coffee machine. "Sunil, meet Fabian Weber from Terahash and Jan Smilovic from Bitcity. These guys have some of the most interesting operations I know."

Fabian shook Sunil's hand. "Dusan told me you're thinking about getting into mining. Good timing to learn from other people's mistakes," he laughed.

Jan pulled up a chair. "And successes too, hopefully. Though Fabian's right, we've all made our share of blunders."

"OK," Dusan said, settling back in his chair, "you wanted real mining stories, not just theory. These guys have lived it."

Sunil nodded, blowing on his coffee. It was too hot to drink just yet. "Yeah, actual examples would help me get it better."

"I'll start with a classic," Fabian said. "There's this guy in Sweden we all know, Mikael. Started real small back in 2016. Just three machines in his garage, nothing fancy."

"And he made it work?" Sunil asked.

"Yeah, because he had two big things going for him," Jan continued. "Sweden's got crazy cheap hydroelectric power. And it's cold most of the year. So his costs were way lower than most people's right from the start."

Fabian took a sip of his coffee, made a face. Still too hot. "So by mid-2017 he'd moved to a small warehouse, with maybe fifty machines running. Then the big crash hit in 2018."

"The one where Bitcoin tanked?"

"Dropped from like twenty thousand to three thousand in less than a year," Dusan nodded. "Total bloodbath. But here's where Mikael got smart. While everyone else was selling their machines cheap and giving up, he was buying."

"Because he could still make money even with the low prices?" Sunil guessed.

"Exactly," Jan said. "His costs were so low that he was still profitable when everyone else was underwater. By 2020 he had like five hundred machines going. Guy's operation is huge now."

A group at the next table erupted in laughter about something, momentarily interrupting them. When it quieted down, Sunil asked, "So what's the lesson there?"

"Know your advantage and double down on it when times get tough," Fabian said. "And don't follow the crowd. When everyone's selling, that might be the time to buy."

Dusan's phone buzzed. He glanced at it, then put it away. "Oh, and now he's dealing with politicians talking about taxing mining operations more. Just shows you can never get too comfortable in this business."

Sunil's coffee had cooled enough to drink now. It was decent, nothing special. "Got any other examples? A different approach maybe?"

"I've got one that's completely different," Jan said, leaning forward. "A woman named Elena in Texas. She used to work in oil and gas, so she knew that at these oil fields, they burn off excess natural gas because it's not worth capturing and moving it anywhere. Just literally burning money."

"Sounds wasteful."

"Super wasteful," Fabian agreed. "So what she did was brilliant. She built these portable mining setups in shipping containers. Takes them right to the oil wells, converts the gas to electricity on site and uses it to power miners."

"That's pretty clever," Sunil said, genuinely impressed.

"Everybody wins," Jan continued. "Oil companies get paid for gas they were wasting. Elena gets basically free electricity. The environment benefits because they're not just burning gas into the air."

Someone had turned on some music in the background. Not too loud, just enough to fill the space. Outside, the sun was getting lower, casting longer shadows through the big windows.

"What about failures?" Sunil asked. "Probably learn more from those sometimes."

"Oh man, seen plenty," Fabian sighed. "People make the same mistakes over and over."

He counted on his fingers. "One, not enough capital. They spend everything on equipment and don't keep cash for electricity, repairs, or rough patches."

"Two, terrible timing," Jan added. "Jumping in when bitcoin's at all-time highs, paying top dollar for equipment, then watching prices crash before they've made back their investment."

"Three, ignoring basic costs," Dusan continued. "Knew a guy who set up in New York City because that's where he lived. Didn't factor in that electricity there costs a fortune. Was losing money from day one."

"Sounds like stuff that would sink any business," Sunil noted.

"That's just it," Fabian nodded. "People get so excited about the tech and the potential money that they forget it's still a business. Need the same fundamentals as any other business."

A waiter came by asking if they wanted refills. They all said yes. The place had gotten busier as evening set in. They'd turned on some lights inside to compensate for the fading daylight.

"Got one more example that's interesting," Jan said when the waiter left. "Two brothers up in Canada. Started mining in 2017, had maybe 200 machines. They were doing OK, but not great because their power costs weren't anything special."

"What did they do differently?" Sunil asked.

"They switched to hosting other people's machines instead of just mining themselves," Fabian explained. "Started charging a monthly fee per machine plus a cut of the mining rewards."

"Changed everything for them," Jan continued. "Suddenly they weren't so exposed to bitcoin price swings. They made money no matter what bitcoin did."

"Diversification," Sunil said. "Like you mentioned before."

"Right. By 2019 they'd grown ten times bigger, mostly hosting other people's hardware," Dusan added. "Still did some mining themselves, but hosting became their main thing."

Their fresh coffees arrived. Outside it was getting dark. They'd turned the inside lights up more now, giving the place a warmer feel. More people had come in, and the noise level had risen.

"So the big lesson there is adapting," Fabian continued. "Mining doesn't stay the same. Market changes, tech changes, regulations change. Got to be willing to pivot when necessary."

Sunil thought about these stories. "Seems like you need some kind of edge, something that makes you different from everyone else trying to mine."

"Exactly," Jan nodded. "Could be cheap power, cold climate, special business model, whatever. But you need something. Days of just plugging in machines and watching money roll in are long gone."

"How do you find out about these successful miners?" Sunil asked. "They publish this stuff?"

"Some do, in articles or at conferences," Fabian said. "But a lot of it is networking. I've visited tons of mining operations over the years.

Always learn something new. Different cooling setups, maintenance tricks, security approaches."

He pulled out his phone and showed Sunil some photos. "See how different they all look? Warehouse here, purpose-built facility there, containers at this oil field."

"Not one correct way to do it," Sunil observed.

"That's why these real examples matter so much," Jan said. "Shows you different paths that can work, helps you figure out one that makes sense for your situation."

The warehouse was fully in evening mode now. Lights all on, music a bit louder, people having drinks rather than working on laptops. The vibe had shifted from workday to social.

Fabian checked his watch. "Actually, I should head out. Got an early meeting tomorrow." He stood up and shook Sunil's hand. "Good luck with your mining journey. Feel free to reach out if you have questions."

"Same here," Jan said, also standing. "Always happy to help someone starting out. Dusan's got my details."

After they left, Dusan turned to Sunil. "See what I mean about networking? Those guys have been around for years, seen everything."

"Think I've had enough Bitcoin talk for today," Dusan said, checking the time on his phone. "Been at it since morning. Want to grab dinner somewhere? There's a place around the corner that's pretty good."

"Yeah, I'm getting hungry," Sunil agreed. "Thanks for introducing me to Fabian and Jan. Makes it feel more real somehow."

"Barely scratched the surface," Dusan said as they stood up. "Mining world keeps changing. What works today might not work in five years."

"How so?" Sunil asked as they headed for the door.

"Well, that gets into where this whole thing is headed," Dusan replied. "Future halvings change the economics. New cooling tech opening up different locations. Chips potentially hitting physical limits."

They stepped outside into the cooler evening air. The street was lit by old-fashioned lamps, showing off Prague's architecture in a different light than during the day.

"Sounds like another big topic," Sunil said as they walked.

"It is," Dusan agreed. "Future of mining is a whole conversation. But let's save that for tomorrow. Right now I just want some food and maybe a quiet drink after."

Walking through the streets, Sunil found himself thinking about everything he'd learned so far. From the technical stuff to the business side to these real examples of people making it work, the picture was getting clearer. But there was still the question of where it was all going, how mining would evolve in coming years.

That was something for tomorrow though. Right now, his stomach was reminding him he hadn't eaten since lunch. The future of Bitcoin mining could wait until morning.

CHAPTER 17
THE FUTURE OF BITCOIN MINING

Sunil woke up to sunlight streaming through the thin hotel curtains. His head was spinning a bit from all the Bitcoin knowledge he'd absorbed over the past couple days. He checked his phone. 9:17 AM. A text from Dusan: "Morning! Breakfast at the hotel then hike up to the castle? Great view and perfect place to talk about the future of mining. Meeting at lobby 10am."

After a quick shower, Sunil headed down to the hotel restaurant. Dusan was already there, working on what looked like his second cup of coffee and scrolling through something on his phone.

"There he is," Dusan said, looking up. "Sleep OK? We covered a lot yesterday."

"Yeah, good," Sunil replied, grabbing some eggs and bread from the buffet. "Taking a bit to process it all though."

The hotel restaurant was half empty, mostly business travellers typing on laptops between bites of breakfast. Outside, it was a clear day, sun shining on the red rooftops of Prague.

"So," Sunil said after taking a few bites, "you mentioned talking about where mining is headed. The future stuff."

"Right," Dusan nodded. "Figured we could cover that today. After seeing how things work now, it's good to understand where it's all going."

"The castle tour is actually perfect for this conversation," he added. "You get to see centuries of history while we talk about what comes next. Plus the walk up there will clear our heads."

After breakfast, they headed out into the morning air. The streets were already filling with tourists, but as they began climbing the hill toward Prague Castle, the crowds thinned out.

"First thing to understand about the future of mining," Dusan said as they walked up a steep street, "is that it's all about efficiency now. Early miners didn't care much about power consumption or optimization. Bitcoin was worth so little that it didn't matter."

"And now?" Sunil asked.

"Now margins are thin, competition is fierce, and every bit of efficiency counts." Dusan wiped some sweat from his forehead. The hill was steeper than it looked. "There's this constant arms race in mining technology."

They passed a small café with outdoor seating. The smell of fresh pastries was tempting, but they kept walking.

"What kind of innovations are happening?" Sunil asked.

"Several major ones," Dusan replied. "First is chip technology. The newest ASICs use 5 nano-meter chips, way smaller and more efficient than older models. Some manufacturers are already working on 3 nano-meter designs."

"That's smaller than a human hair, right?"

"Way smaller. We're talking atomic scale," Dusan said. "Problem is, we're approaching the physical limits of silicon. Can't go much smaller without dealing with quantum effects that make chips unstable."

They paused at a viewpoint, looking out over the city. Red rooftops spread out below them, church spires poking up here and there. The Vltava River curved through the middle with bridges crossing at various points.

"Beautiful," Sunil remarked.

"It is," Dusan agreed. "OK so chip technology is one innovation path. Another big one is cooling. Traditional air cooling is being replaced by more advanced methods."

"Like what we saw at your friend's place?"

"That was immersion cooling, where the machines are submerged in non-conductive fluid," Dusan explained. "But there's also hydro cooling, which uses water or other liquids in closed loop systems to carry heat away from the miners."

They continued up the hill, passing other tourists who were stopping to take photos of the view. The castle was visible now, massive stone walls looming above them.

"What's the difference between them?" Sunil asked.

"Hydro cooling is more targeted, cooling specific hot spots on the miners. Immersion cooling submerges the whole machine. Both let you push the miners harder than air cooling."

"So they're more efficient?"

"Well, efficiency actually drops a bit with both methods," Dusan clarified. "But here's the thing, you can overclock the machines much more aggressively. So you get lower efficiency per hash, but way more total hashes from each machine."

"Plus the machines last longer because there's less thermal stress and no dust problems with either method."

They reached a plateau area before the final approach to the castle. It was crowded with tour groups following guides with little flags. They found a less busy spot near a wall.

"Then there's something completely different," Dusan continued. "Heat recycling. Mining produces tons of waste heat. Traditionally that's just vented outside, total waste. Now companies are capturing that heat for other uses."

"Like what?"

"Heating buildings, greenhouses, even industrial processes. There's a mining operation in Canada that heats a whole block of apartments. Another in Norway that dries lumber for a wood processing plant."

"So all these innovations are about pushing performance," Sunil noted. "What about Bitcoin itself? Is that changing?"

"That's the interesting thing about Bitcoin," Dusan said. "The protocol itself barely changes. The predictability of the system is one of its key features, plus the fact that the code is hardly changeable. Any major changes need massive consensus from the network."

"But there are some potential changes being discussed that would affect mining," he continued.

"Such as?"

"The biggest one is probably Stratum V2. It's a new mining protocol that gives more control to individual miners rather than pool operators. Makes things more decentralised, more private, and more efficient."

"Wait, isn't that similar to what we talked about with Ocean a few days ago? That DATUM thing?"

"Exactly!" Dusan smiled. "DATUM is Ocean's implementation of giving miners more control over block construction. Stratum V2 takes that concept even further across the whole mining ecosystem. Both are moving in the same direction of putting power back in miners' hands instead of pool operators."

A tour group moved past them, tour guide speaking loudly in German. They waited for them to pass before continuing.

"Another hot topic is the growth of Bitcoin usage and how it affects miners," Dusan said. "More users mean more transactions, which means more fees for miners. This is becoming increasingly important as block subsidies decrease with each halving."

They started walking again, heading toward the castle entrance. Stone archways and medieval architecture surrounded them, a stark contrast to their conversation about cutting edge technology.

"Speaking of that," Sunil said, "isn't that a problem long term? Eventually the subsidies will be basically zero, right?"

"Well, let me clarify something first," Dusan said as they walked. "People often confuse block subsidy with block reward. The total block reward is subsidy plus fees. The subsidy is what gets halved every four years and will eventually go to zero, that's known and built into the system."

"So the subsidy disappears, but fees could make up for it?"

"That's the theory," Dusan nodded. "The subsidy will be basically zero in over a hundred years. By then, the idea is that transaction fees alone should sustain mining. Some people worry about it, others think the market will sort itself out."

They joined the line for tickets to enter the castle. The queue moved fairly quickly, and soon they were inside the massive complex. They wandered through courtyards and past historic buildings, finding a quiet bench in a garden area.

"There's another huge trend changing mining," Dusan said as they sat down. "Renewable energy. It's reshaping the whole landscape."

"I thought miners just looked for the cheapest power, regardless of source," Sunil said.

"Historically, yes. But that's changing for a couple reasons. First, renewables are often the cheapest option now. Solar and wind prices have dropped dramatically. In many places, they're cheaper than fossil fuels."

"Second, there's increasing pressure on miners to be environmentally responsible. Whether from public opinion, investors, or regulations, the push toward clean energy is real."

A church bell rang somewhere in the distance. Birds were chirping in the trees around the garden. Despite being in the middle of a popular tourist attraction, this particular spot was surprisingly peaceful.

"What about grid tied versus off grid mining?" Sunil asked. "You mentioned both exist."

"That's another interesting development," Dusan replied. "Traditional mining operations connect to the power grid. But there's a growing trend toward off grid mining using stranded or wasted energy sources."

"Solar farms in remote desert areas. Hydroelectric dams during spring melt when they produce excess power. Wind farms at night when demand is low. Oil fields with flared gas. All places where power is available but can't be used locally or transmitted to population centres."

"Bitcoin mining is unique because it can be placed anywhere power exists. It doesn't need to be near cities or transportation hubs."

Sunil watched a butterfly land on a nearby flower. "It's kind of ironic. Bitcoin gets criticized for energy use, but it might actually help the transition to renewables."

"Exactly," Dusan said, nodding vigorously. "Renewable projects often struggle with intermittency and capacity factors. Solar only produces during daylight, wind is inconsistent, hydro has seasonal variations."

"Traditional power users need constant, reliable electricity. But Bitcoin miners can ramp up when excess power is available and shut down when it's not. Perfect flexible load for renewable energy."

They got up and continued their tour of the castle grounds, passing through grand halls with vaulted ceilings and ancient tapestries.

"What about the criticism that Bitcoin just uses too much energy, period?" Sunil asked as they examined a display of medieval weapons.

"Complex question," Dusan said. "Bitcoin does use a lot of energy, no denying that. But you have to ask what that energy is achieving. If you believe Bitcoin provides value as a global, censorship resistant monetary system, then the energy use makes sense."

"Plus, energy use doesn't equal environmental impact. A Bitcoin miner running on solar has very different environmental consequences than one running on coal, even if they use the same amount of electricity."

They emerged from the castle and found another viewpoint, even higher than before. The entire city of Prague stretched out before them, a mix of ancient and modern architecture under the clear blue sky.

"So where do you see mining in ten years?" Sunil asked, taking in the panoramic view.

"More specialized, more efficient, more integrated with energy systems," Dusan replied without hesitation. "The easy money days are over. Future miners will need to be sophisticated operations with expertise in energy, technology, finance, and increasingly, environmental management."

"Large scale mining will likely consolidate around regions with optimal conditions: cool climates, cheap renewable energy, favourable regulations. While small operations will focus on utilizing stranded energy resources that larger players can't efficiently capture."

"And what about people wanting to get into mining?" Sunil asked. "Will there still be opportunities?"

"Absolutely," Dusan nodded. "But they'll need to be smarter about it. The path to success will require more knowledge, more planning, and more creativity than before."

He glanced at Sunil with a slight smile. "Actually, that brings up something I've been thinking about since we started these conversations."

"What's that?"

"Well, you've been absorbing all this mining knowledge pretty quickly. And you mentioned looking for something besides sailing. Have you considered becoming a mining expert yourself?"

"Me?" Sunil looked surprised. "I've only been learning about this for a few days."

"Everyone starts somewhere," Dusan shrugged. "And you've got skills that transfer well. Technical knowledge from ships, problem solving experience, international perspective. Those are valuable in the mining world."

Sunil looked out over the city, considering the idea. It wasn't something he'd seriously thought about, but now that Dusan mentioned it...

"What would that even look like?" he asked. "Becoming a mining expert, I mean."

"That's a whole conversation in itself," Dusan replied. "There's different paths depending on your interests and strengths. But if you're curious, we can talk about it over lunch. I know a place near here with a great view and even better food."

As they started down the hill from the castle, Sunil found himself genuinely intrigued by the possibility. From casual curiosity to potential career path in just a few days? Life takes strange turns sometimes.

The future of mining was clearly complex and evolving, but maybe that's what made it interesting. And the idea of being part of that future, of developing expertise in this growing field, was something worth exploring further.

"Lunch sounds good," he said. "And yeah, I'd like to hear more about that expert path."

CHAPTER 18
BECOMING A BITCOIN MINING EXPERT

The restaurant Dusan picked was on a hillside with a terrace overlooking the city. Not super fancy, but the kind of place locals went for good food at reasonable prices. They got a table right by the railing with a view that rivalled the one from the castle.

"Man, you weren't kidding about the view," Sunil said as they settled in. The waiter brought them water and menus in both Czech and English.

"Food's even better," Dusan replied. "Try the pork knuckle if you're hungry. It's their specialty."

After they ordered, Sunil brought the conversation back to what Dusan had mentioned at the castle. "So you really think I could become some kind of mining expert? I barely know anything yet."

"Everyone starts somewhere," Dusan shrugged. "But yeah, I do. You pick things up quickly, ask good questions, and you've got practical experience with complex systems from your ship work."

"But how would I even go about it? There's no mining school or certification, right?"

"Not officially, no," Dusan agreed. "It's not like being a doctor or lawyer. But that doesn't mean there isn't a path."

Their drinks arrived, some kind of local lemonade that Dusan had recommended. It was tart and refreshing after their walk down from the castle.

"The most important thing for becoming a mining expert is constant learning," Dusan continued. "This industry changes so fast that what you know today might be outdated in six months."

"That sounds exhausting," Sunil frowned.

"It can be," Dusan nodded. "But there are ways to manage it. You gotta be strategic about your information sources."

He pulled out his phone and showed Sunil a list of bookmarked websites. "These are my go-to sources. Mining-specific forums like Bitcoin Talk's mining section. The Bitcoin dev mailing list. Mining hardware manufacturers' update pages. A few key Twitter accounts from mining operators and developers."

"Seems like a lot to keep up with," Sunil noted.

"You develop a system," Dusan said, putting his phone away. "Set aside time each week to catch up on developments. I usually do an hour every Sunday morning. Skim everything, deep dive only on what's relevant to your operation or interests."

Their food arrived, steaming plates with generous portions. Sunil had gone with Dusan's recommendation, and the pork knuckle was massive, falling off the bone.

"This is amazing," Sunil said after his first bite.

"Told you," Dusan grinned, digging into his own meal. "So, continuing education. Beyond just staying updated on news, there's hands-on learning."

"Like what?"

"Building test rigs. Experimenting with different firmware. Setting up small-scale cooling systems." Dusan paused to eat a few bites. "Nothing teaches you like doing it yourself and making mistakes on a small scale before advising others."

A family at the next table was celebrating something, clinking glasses and taking photos. The terrace was filling up with the lunch crowd, a mix of tourists and locals enjoying the sunny day.

"What about communities?" Sunil asked. "You mentioned forums, but are there like, actual people you can talk to about this stuff?"

"That's crucial," Dusan nodded emphatically. "Mining can seem super technical, but it's actually a people business at heart. Networking is how you get the really valuable information."

"There are mining conferences all over the world now. Some Bitcoin-specific, others more general crypto events with mining tracks. Those are goldmines for connections and insider knowledge."

"Plus local meetups like the one we went to. Every major city with tech people has some kind of crypto group. Even if it's just a few folks meeting at a bar once a month."

Sunil took a drink of his lemonade. "What about online? I'm on ships for half the year, remember?"

"Plenty of online communities too. Discord servers, Telegram groups, private Slack channels. Some are open to anyone, others you need an invitation." Dusan wiped his mouth with a napkin. "I can add you to a few good ones."

"The key thing with communities, whether online or in person, is to start by listening and learning. Don't jump in asking basic questions right away. Lurk, absorb, then gradually join the conversation when you have something to contribute."

"Sounds like dating advice," Sunil laughed.

"Kind of is," Dusan grinned. "You're building relationships, not just gathering information. The best opportunities come through people who know and trust you."

They ate in comfortable silence for a few minutes, enjoying the food and the view. A church bell rang somewhere in the city below. Small boats moved along the river, looking tiny from their hillside perch.

"What about resources specifically for consultants?" Sunil asked eventually. "If I wanted to go that route."

"Good question," Dusan said. "Consulting requires a different toolset beyond just technical knowledge."

He counted off on his fingers. "You need documentation templates: assessment forms, audit checklists, proposal formats, contract templates. Saves tons of time to have these ready to go."

"Then there's analysis tools. Software for modelling different mining scenarios based on variables like electricity cost, bitcoin price projections, hardware efficiency. I use a custom spreadsheet I've built over years, but there are some decent ones available online too."

"Do you share your clients with other consultants? Like referring work?"

"Sometimes," Dusan nodded. "I have a network of specialists I bring in for certain aspects. Like, I know a guy who's incredible with cooling system design. Another who specializes in power contracts. An attorney who handles mining-specific legal issues."

A waiter came by to check on them and clear some empty plates. Dusan ordered coffee for both of them.

"And how do you stay competitive?" Sunil asked when the waiter left. "Seems like more people must be getting into this consulting thing as mining grows."

"Definitely getting more crowded," Dusan agreed. "A few years ago I was one of maybe a dozen people doing this seriously. Now there's hundreds."

"So you specialize, go deeper rather than broader. Find your specific angle based on your background and strengths."

"Like what?"

"Well, for me, it's facility design and operational efficiency. Others focus on different niches: financial modelling, security systems, regulatory compliance, renewable energy integration."

Their coffees arrived, served in small cups with sugar on the side.

"With your background," Dusan continued, "you might focus on something like redundant systems and failover protocols. Ships can't just stop in the middle of the ocean when something breaks. That mindset is valuable in mining too."

"Or maybe international deployments, since you've worked all over the world. Understanding different electrical standards, import regulations, climate considerations."

Sunil nodded slowly, considering this. "I can see how that might work."

"Beyond specializing, staying competitive means being visible," Dusan added. "Writing articles, speaking at events, creating case studies of successful projects. Not just to get clients, but to establish credibility in the community."

"And constantly learning new skills. Like right now I'm studying machine learning to improve predictive maintenance for mining operations. Identifying patterns that might indicate a component is going to fail before it actually does."

They finished their coffees, and Dusan signalled for the check. The lunch crowd had thinned somewhat, leaving the terrace quieter than before.

"It's a lot to take in," Sunil admitted. "But broken down like this, it seems more doable than I first thought."

"That's the thing about any complex field," Dusan said. "Looks impossible from the outside. But once you're in it, taking it step by step, it's manageable."

The waiter brought their bill, and they both reached for their wallets. Dusan waved Sunil off. "I got this one."

"Thanks," Sunil said. "For lunch and all the advice."

"No problem. Actually, I was thinking we should visit a place this afternoon that might interest you, given what we've been talking about."

"What kind of place?"

"It's a data centre outside the city that's been converted to partially run on renewable energy. They've got an interesting setup where they balance between grid power and their own solar array depending on electricity prices."

"Sounds cool," Sunil nodded. "Is it a mining operation?"

"Not primarily," Dusan replied as they got up to leave. "But they do have a mining section that acts as a load balancer for their power systems. It's a great example of how mining fits into broader energy markets."

"Energy markets?" Sunil raised an eyebrow. "That's a whole other topic, isn't it?"

"It is," Dusan agreed. "And increasingly important for anyone in mining. Understanding how electricity is priced, how grid systems work, where the cheapest power is found, and why. That knowledge can be the difference between a profitable operation and a failed one."

They made their way out of the restaurant and back onto the winding street that led down the hill. The afternoon sun was warm, but a breeze kept it comfortable.

"We'll need to grab my car," Dusan said. "The data centre is about thirty minutes outside Prague. But I think you'll find it worth the trip. Shows a whole different side of how mining integrates with energy systems."

As they walked, Sunil found himself genuinely interested in seeing this facility. The technical aspects of mining were fascinating enough, but the bigger picture of how it interacted with energy markets and infrastructure was starting to seem equally important. It was yet another piece of the complex puzzle he was gradually assembling in his mind.

CHAPTER 19
UNDERSTANDING THE ENERGY MARKETS

The data centre was about a half hour drive outside Prague, a modern glass and metal building surrounded by fields with a large solar array visible behind it. Not what Sunil had expected at all.

"A friend of mine is the operations manager here," Dusan explained as they pulled into the parking lot. "He's arranged for a few people to talk to us about different energy markets. Figured it would be more interesting than just me lecturing you."

Dusan had called ahead, so they were expected. A security guard checked their IDs and gave them visitor badges before directing them inside. The lobby was sleek and minimalist, with a reception desk staffed by a young woman who greeted Dusan by name.

"They're waiting for you in the conference room," she said, gesturing toward a hallway. "Your guests from the video call are already connected."

The conference room had a large table with a screen on one wall showing two video feeds. One showed a dark skinned man with a bright smile, the other a serious looking guy with blonde hair.

"Perfect timing," Dusan said as they entered. "Sunil, meet Kal and Fabian. They're joining us virtually to talk about energy markets in their countries."

The man on the left feed waved. "Hello from Ethiopia," he said. "Kal Kassa. I'm founder of a Bitcoin education company called BitcoinBirr. I act as advisor for a lot of companies that operate in Ethiopia and publish educational content for Ethiopian markets."

"And I'm Fabian from Finland," said the other man. "Head of Hashrate at Terahash. space. We specialise in integrating Bitcoin data centres into energy infrastructure."

A door opened and a man in jeans and a company polo shirt came in. "Sorry I'm late," he said, shaking hands with both of them. "The tour ran long. I'm Martin, operations manager here."

They all sat down, and Martin brought up some slides on the screen next to the video feeds.

"So we're talking energy markets today," Dusan began. "Figured we'd go through a few different countries to show how varied the landscape is. Sunil's interested in possibly getting into mining consulting, and understanding energy is crucial for that."

Martin nodded. "Makes sense. Want me to start with our setup here as an example?"

"Perfect," Dusan agreed.

Martin clicked to a diagram showing how their facility was connected to both the grid and their solar array. "We're what's called a hybrid system. Primary power comes from the grid, but we supplement with our own solar during peak production hours. Our Bitcoin mining section acts as a flexible load."

"Meaning?" Sunil asked.

"We can dial it up when we have excess solar power, or dial it down when grid electricity is expensive," Martin explained. "Unlike most of our data operations which need consistent power, mining can be throttled up or down as needed."

"That's becoming a major trend worldwide," Dusan added. "Mining as a flexible power consumer that can balance grids or monetise otherwise wasted energy."

"Exactly," Martin nodded. "But energy markets vary dramatically by country. That's why I asked Dusan to bring in Kal and Fabian to give you a broader perspective."

Kal's face enlarged on the screen as he began speaking. "Ethiopia is a really interesting case study for mining. We have abundant hydroelectric power, with more dams being built every year. The government has been actively trying to monetise this energy because we generate more than our domestic economy can use currently."

"What's the process like for getting started there?" Sunil asked.

"Well, it starts with getting permission," Kal explained. "You need pre-import approval through a single-window tool that integrates various governmental departments before you can bring in mining equipment. INSA, Customs, and the Investment Commission all have to sign off before you can even ship miners from China or Hong Kong."

"INSA?" Sunil asked.

"Information Network Security Administration," Kal clarified. "Once equipment arrives, there's about a two week validation process, sometimes up to three weeks maximum. INSA does their validation for free, but there's a 3% flat customs fee."

"What about electricity costs?" Dusan prompted.

"That's the big attraction," Kal smiled. "Ethiopian Electric Power offers PPAs at 3.14 cents USD per kilowatt hour. Add 15% VAT and a 0.5% regulatory fee, so total taxes are 15.5%, and you're at about 3.63 cents all in just for the energy."

"That's incredibly cheap," Sunil noted.

"Exactly why we're seeing a mining boom there," Dusan nodded. "But there are complications with the business structures, right Kal?"

"Yes, there are essentially two types of players in Ethiopia," Kal continued. "First type are those who've directly acquired PPAs. They form local companies, lease land, and develop their own sites for air cooling or hydro cooling or both. They handle their own operations and maintenance."

"The second type are foreign companies that don't want to form Ethiopian entities. They partner with local companies that have PPAs and handle ground operations. The foreign companies pay for infrastructure and offer mining as a service on top."

"What's the advantage of the second approach?" Sunil asked.

"Two-step validation," Kal explained. "The ground operations team isn't just supervised by the local company, but also advised by the foreign company's operations people. Generally makes operations smoother, though typical all-in hosting prices range from 5 to 6 cents."

"Any major challenges with ownership?" Dusan asked.

"Definitely," Kal nodded. "The local company that imports the miners is legally the owner. If you're not happy with hosting services, you have limited options. For relocation, you need cooperation from the current hosting company for import invoices and customs declarations, plus asset appraisal and repaying the 3% import tax."

"And for exporting?" Sunil asked.

"Possible, but complex. If you have a lot of miners, you should do a joint agreement with the local company where ownership stays with you. Then either party can ship out the miners since legally they belong to the local company anyway."

"One important restriction," Kal added. "Local companies offering hosting services cannot mine themselves. They can only offer hosting."

"So as a client, what are your options?" Dusan asked.

"Two main choices," Kal replied. "Choose a company that has the PPA directly, and you might get slightly lower hosting fees. Or choose an aggregator partner company with two-step validation, where operations are always supervised and generally smoother because two groups are involved."

Martin clicked to a new slide showing a map of Europe. "Let's shift to Finland. Fabian, want to take it from here?"

The blonde man nodded. "Finland is part of what we call the Nord Pool, a common energy market for all Scandinavian countries. We have three main ways to procure energy: spot prices, futures, and PPAs."

"Spot prices change hourly and can be highly volatile," Fabian continued. "Most serious miners avoid them because you can't plan properly. Futures and PPAs make more sense for stable operations."

"Can you explain the futures approach?" Sunil asked.

"Absolutely. The beauty of futures is predictability," Fabian said, pulling up the Nasdaq website on his screen. "You can lock in prices quarterly or yearly basis. This is incredibly beneficial because spot prices can be very high and variable, which isn't conducive for mining."

"Why is that so important?" Sunil prompted.

"Because in mining, it's great to know your fixed price in advance. You can do your planning accordingly," Fabian explained. "That's why it's best to lock your future prices, either quarterly or yearly."

"What are current prices like?" Dusan asked.

"The energy price you see on the Nasdaq website ranges between roughly 28 to 35 euros per megawatt hour right now," Fabian replied. "But that's just the starting point."

European Market

Product Series	Bid	Ask	Last	+/-	%	High
ENOFUTBLYR-26	38.25	38.40	38.40	+0.25	+0.65%	38.45
ENOFUTBLYR-27	38.20	38.45		-0.10	-0.26%	
ENOFUTBLYR-28	38.30	39.00		+0.20	+0.51%	
ENOFUTBLYR-30	39.50	41.95		-2.92	-7.17%	
SYBERFUTBLYR-26				+9.50	+126.66%	
SYHELFUTBLYR-26	5.70	6.40		-0.10	-1.61%	
SYKRIFUTBLYR-26						
SYOSLFUTBLYR-26	11.50			+0.20	+1.66%	

"There are two more costs to consider," he continued. "System price, which depends on how much capacity you take, and transmission fees. Once we add all this together, it comes to 65 to 75 euros per megawatt hour, depending on which area of Finland you're operating from."

"That sounds expensive," Sunil noted, concerned.

"You might think so, but that's the brilliant part about Finland," Fabian said, his face lighting up. "Finland offers two huge advantages that bring costs way down."

"First is the demand response program. When we participate with 100% uptime and no curtailment, we get 6 to 7 euros back per megawatt hour."

"And the second advantage?" Sunil asked.

"Heat reuse from hydro mining," Fabian explained. "We can resell that heat and get 25 to 35 euros back per megawatt hour."

Fabian pulled up a calculator on his screen. "Let me show you the maths. Say we start at 70 euros per megawatt hour total cost. Subtract 6.5 euros for demand response, subtract 30 euros for heat sales. Our effective cost drops to just 33.5 euros per megawatt hour."

"That's competitive with much cheaper regions," Sunil said, impressed.

"Exactly," Dusan nodded. "But there's a limitation, right Fabian?"

"Yes, when we opt for district heating, there's a constraint. We cannot operate a site larger than 2 or 3 megawatts. So there's definitely an opportunity, but with a size limitation."

"What about demand response specifically?" Sunil asked. "How does that work?"

"Let me explain demand response properly," Fabian said. "Demand response means moving electricity use from times when demand and prices are high to cheaper times, or temporarily adjusting usage to keep the grid balanced. Think of the electrical grid as a big system that brings electricity to your home."

"In Finland, our Transmission System Operator, Fingrid, decides the hours for demand response. They use it to balance the energy market and ensure reliable electricity supply. They're responsible for managing the grid and balancing supply and demand."

"So how does the compensation work?" Sunil asked.

"Here's where it gets interesting," Fabian continued. "Last year in 2024, average demand response program hours were 8,760 hours in the year, and they paid 9 euros per megawatt hour as compensation for participants."

"That's the full year?"

"Exactly. Let's assume we have 8,000 hours in 2025 for our calculations. That would be 8,000 hours times 9 euros per megawatt hour, which equals 72,000 euros per year per megawatt."

"But there's a catch," he added. "About 20% of the compensation is taken by the utility company, so you actually get 57,600 euros per megawatt."

"Can you break that down to a more practical level?" Dusan prompted.

"Sure. Assuming we have 8,760 total hours in the year, and let's say we have a 1 megawatt operation, which is 1,000 kilowatts. The demand response payment per kilowatt hour works out to 57,600 divided by 8,760 hours times 1,000 kilowatts, which equals about 0.66 euro cents per kilowatt hour."

"That's a rough calculation, but it gives you the idea of the financial benefit," Fabian concluded.

"And the heat reuse?" Dusan prompted.

"The heat generated from Bitcoin mining can be supplied to district heating companies or directly to end users like hotels, residential buildings, or industrial facilities," Fabian continued. "In Finland, average district heat prices for apartment buildings were 91.2 euros per megawatt hour in January 2023, ranging from 52.8 to 137.5 depending on the company."

"Even if you sell heat for just 25 euros per megawatt hour, that's still a significant cost reduction."

"Plus, there are legal ways where you get your VAT back," Fabian added. "So while there's a 25.5% VAT, it doesn't impact cash flow for long."

Martin checked his watch. "We've got about twenty more minutes before I need to get back to the floor. Dusan, want to cover some other markets quickly?"

"Sure," Dusan nodded. "Let me talk about UAE, specifically Abu Dhabi and Dubai."

He pulled out his phone and showed Sunil some photos of desert facilities with solar panels. "UAE is interesting because on paper, it shouldn't be competitive for mining. Regular electricity rates are around 10 cents per kilowatt hour, plus costs for land and infrastructure."

"So why is there mining happening there?" Sunil asked.

"Two reasons," Dusan replied. "First, some companies just want a UAE business registration for tax benefits. No tax up to 375,000 AED, about 102,000 USD, and only 9% after that."

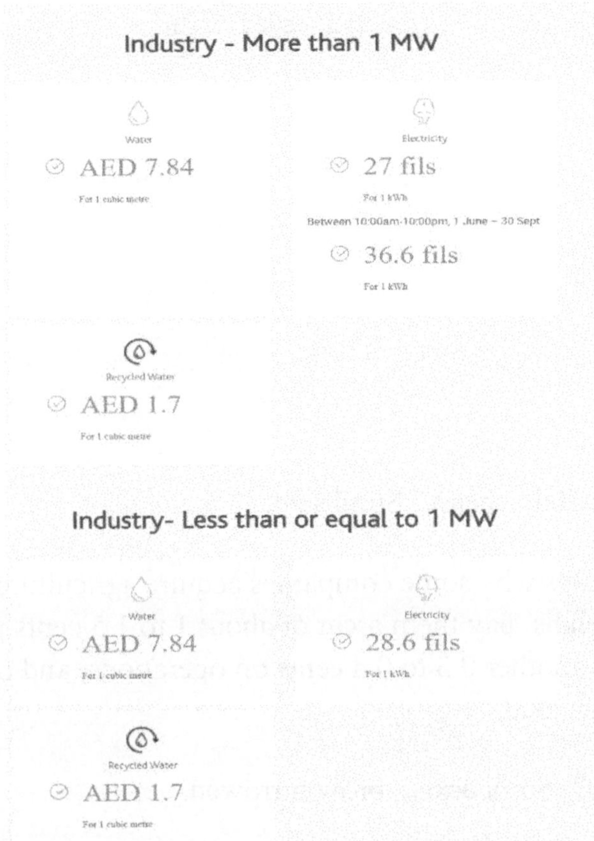

"But the real mining happens because of a loophole. TAQA, the Abu Dhabi energy company, offers subsidised agricultural rates of just 0.045 AED per kilowatt hour, which is about 1.2 cents USD."

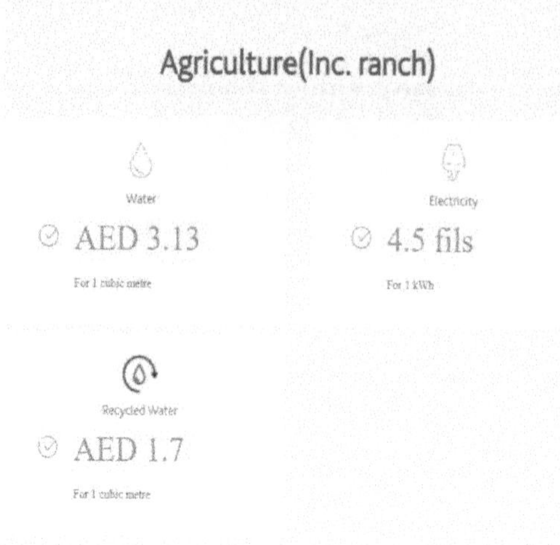

"That's incredibly cheap," Sunil said.

"Yes, and that's why some companies acquire agricultural land from locals or sheikhs, pay them a cut of about 1 to 1.5 cents per kilowatt hour, spend another 0.3 to 0.4 cents on operations, and offer hosting at 5 to 6 cents total."

"Is that legal?" Sunil asked, brow furrowed.

"Grey area," Dusan admitted. "ADAA, the Abu Dhabi Agriculture Authority, has technically banned crypto mining on farms. The subsidised rates are meant for agriculture only. Some companies claim they're backed by sheikhs, but don't have proper documentation."

"And to legally mine in the UAE, you need a trade licence, right?" Martin asked.

"Exactly," Dusan nodded. "Either from DMCC, Dubai Multi Commodities Centre, or ADDED, Abu Dhabi Department of Economic Development. But ADDED has stopped issuing licences for crypto mining activities, so only DMCC is an option now."

Sunil took notes on his phone. "What about Russia? I've heard there's a lot of mining there."

"Russia is complicated," Dusan said, his expression more serious. "They have some of the cheapest electricity in the world, especially in Siberia where rates can be below 2 cents. Plus a cold climate that reduces cooling costs."

"But," he held up a finger, "there are significant regulatory and political risks. Rules change frequently, and international sanctions complicate equipment imports and fund transfers."

"Would you recommend it?" Sunil asked.

"For most Western operators, no," Dusan shook his head. "The risks outweigh the benefits. But local Russian operators can do well if they have the right connections."

"And the US?" Sunil prompted. "That's a major mining centre now, right?"

"Absolutely," Dusan nodded. "Especially Texas, which has become a global mining hub. What makes Texas attractive is its deregulated energy market, abundant natural gas, growing renewable sector, and relatively friendly regulatory environment."

"Some miners in Texas actually get paid to shut down during grid stress times," Martin added. "They act as a flexible load that helps stabilise the grid."

"Exactly," Dusan agreed. "And in states like Washington, New York, and Montana, hydroelectric power has attracted miners. Though New York has implemented some restrictions recently."

"Wyoming is also emerging as a mining friendly state," Martin noted. "They've passed several laws specifically supporting the industry."

"The US landscape varies state by state," Dusan continued. "Some welcome mining, others restrict it. Electricity prices range from about 3 cents to over 10 cents depending on location and energy source."

Kal and Fabian's feeds showed them checking the time. "We should probably wrap up," Kal said. "Any specific questions about Ethiopia before I go?"

"Just one," Sunil said. "What would you say is the biggest misconception about mining in Ethiopia?"

"That it's unsafe or unstable," Kal replied without hesitation. "Ethiopia has had political challenges, yes, but the mining sector has been remarkably stable because the government recognises its value for monetising excess energy capacity."

Fabian nodded in agreement. "And for Finland, the misconception is that our electricity is expensive. While base rates might look higher than some places, once you factor in demand response and heat reuse, we're competitive with anywhere in the world."

"Great points," Dusan said. "And that brings up something important. Energy markets aren't static. Prices change, regulations evolve, new machine generations come online. A good mining consultant needs to stay current on all this."

Martin stood up, indicating their time was ending. "I hope this was helpful. I can show you a bit of our facility before you head out if you'd like."

After thanking Kal and Fabian for their time, they followed Martin on a brief tour. The mining section was sealed off behind glass walls, rows of ASICs humming away, with monitors showing power consumption and hash rates. Most interesting to Sunil was the control system that automatically adjusted mining output based on solar production and grid power prices.

Back in the car heading toward Prague, Sunil was quiet for a while, processing everything he'd learned.

"It's a lot to take in," Dusan said, glancing over at him. "Energy markets are complex, and they're just one piece of the mining puzzle."

"I can see why understanding them is so important though," Sunil replied. "The difference between profitable and unprofitable seems to often come down to electricity costs and the regulatory environment."

"Exactly," Dusan nodded. "And it's knowledge most people don't have, which makes it valuable."

The late afternoon sun cast long shadows as they drove back toward the city. Prague's skyline came into view, the castle silhouetted against the darkening sky.

"So," Dusan said after a comfortable silence, "if you're serious about becoming a mining expert, there's one more thing we should talk about."

"What's that?" Sunil asked.

"Building your personal brand," Dusan replied. "If you want clients to find you and trust your expertise, you need visibility in the industry."

"Personal brand?" Sunil laughed. "That sounds like influencer stuff."

"Not quite," Dusan shook his head with a smile. "It's about establishing credibility and a professional reputation. You've got a unique background and perspective. Leveraging that could help you stand out in an increasingly crowded field."

"I wouldn't even know where to start," Sunil admitted.

"That's what we can talk about over dinner," Dusan said as they entered the city. "I know some people who've built successful professional brands in the mining space. There are specific strategies that work well in this industry."

As they navigated through Prague's evening traffic, Sunil found himself mentally reviewing everything he'd learned over the past few days. From the technical basics of mining to business models, market dynamics, and now energy economics, the pieces were starting to fit together into a comprehensive picture.

And perhaps, with the right approach to building his professional presence, he could turn this newfound knowledge into a viable career path. That was certainly worth discussing over their final dinner in Prague.

CHAPTER 20
BUILDING YOUR CONSULTANCY BRAND

For their final dinner in Prague, Dusan took Sunil to a restaurant on the top floor of a building near the Old Town Square. The place had floor to ceiling windows with a panoramic view of the city, now lit up against the night sky. The Prague Castle glowed on the hill across the river, and the Charles Bridge was visible in the distance, its statues illuminated by old fashioned lamps.

"Figured we should end with a view of everything you've seen this week," Dusan said as they were seated at a window table.

"It's been quite a journey," Sunil replied, looking out at the cityscape. "Hard to believe it's only been five days since I got here."

"Time flies when your brain is melting from Bitcoin knowledge," Dusan laughed. The waiter came by with menus and water, then left them to decide.

"So," Dusan continued, "personal branding. You seemed skeptical in the car."

"Just the term sounds kind of... I don't know, influencer-ish," Sunil admitted. "Not really my style."

"Forget the term then," Dusan shrugged. "Think of it as building professional credibility and visibility. Same concept, less cringe factor."

The waiter returned and they ordered drinks, a local craft beer for Dusan and a glass of Czech wine for Sunil. Once he'd left, Dusan leaned forward.

"Look, here's the thing. There are tons of smart people in mining. But the ones who get the consulting gigs, the speaking spots, the high paying roles? They're the ones who are visible. Who have established themselves as experts."

"I get that," Sunil nodded. "But I'm literally just learning all this stuff. Feels weird to position myself as some kind of expert."

"You don't start claiming you're the world's top authority," Dusan smiled. "You start by sharing what you do know, from your unique perspective."

Their drinks arrived, and they took a moment to look over the food menu. After ordering, Dusan pulled out his phone.

"Let me show you something," he said, scrolling through Twitter. "This guy, Thomas. Three years ago he was a complete newbie asking basic questions in mining forums."

He showed Sunil a profile with thousands of followers. "Now he's a respected voice in mining infrastructure design. Consults for operations all over Europe."

"What changed?" Sunil asked, genuinely curious.

"He started documenting his learning journey," Dusan replied. "Posted about mistakes he made setting up his first miners. Shared cooling solutions he developed for his small operation. Created a simple guide about electrical safety for home miners."

"And that was enough to build a reputation?"

"Over time, yes. He was consistent, focused on adding real value, and always careful to stay within his actual knowledge base. Never pretended to know more than he did."

Their appetizers arrived, some kind of local cheese with bread and a small salad. The food looked delicious, and they both dug in.

"So where would I even start?" Sunil asked between bites. "I don't exactly have a mining operation to document."

"Start with what makes you unique," Dusan said. "You've got this background in ship engineering and international shipping. There are angles there, no one else has explored much."

"Like what?"

"Like... maritime industry power management lessons that apply to mining. Or logistical challenges of international equipment shipping, which you understand better than most miners. Or redundant system design principles from ships that could improve mining operations."

Sunil nodded slowly, considering this. "That actually makes some sense."

"The key is finding that intersection of mining and your existing expertise," Dusan continued. "That's your unique angle."

"OK, so I have an angle. Then what?"

"Then you need platforms," Dusan said. "Social media is the obvious starting point. LinkedIn, Twitter, YouTube if you're comfortable on camera."

"I've got LinkedIn but barely use it," Sunil admitted. "And I think I made a Twitter account years ago but forgot the password."

"LinkedIn is probably your best starting point for mining consulting. More professional, business focused." Dusan pulled out his phone again. "Here, look at my LinkedIn activity."

He showed Sunil a feed of posts about mining facility designs, energy efficiency case studies, and occasional photos from site visits or conferences.

"I post about twice a week," Dusan explained. "Mix of technical content, project highlights, and industry news commentary. Not trying to go viral or anything, just consistently showing up in my network's feed with valuable content."

"And that brings in clients?"

"Not directly, usually. But when someone in my network needs mining expertise, I'm top of mind because they've seen my posts. Or they recommend me to someone else because they perceive me as knowledgeable in that area."

Their main courses arrived, traditional Czech dishes with a modern twist. The restaurant had a warm buzz of conversation around them, mostly what sounded like business dinners and tourists splurging on a nice meal.

"What about Twitter?" Sunil asked after they'd had a few bites. "Seems like there's a lot of crypto people there."

"Twitter is great for connecting with the broader Bitcoin community," Dusan nodded. "More casual, more immediate. Good for networking with other miners, keeping up with trends, joining conversations about industry news."

"You don't need to tweet fifty times a day. Even just sharing thoughtful comments on major mining developments or helping answer questions builds your reputation over time."

Sunil took a sip of his wine. "You mentioned writing too. Like blogs or something?"

"Content creation is huge for establishing expertise," Dusan agreed. "Could be blog posts, white papers, guides, case studies, whatever format works for you."

"I'm not much of a writer," Sunil frowned.

"Doesn't have to be fancy," Dusan shrugged. "Technical people value clarity over style. A straightforward guide about, say, 'Shipping Mining Equipment Internationally: Logistics and Regulatory Considerations' could be incredibly valuable to the community."

"And where would I publish something like that?"

"Start with Medium or a simple personal website. Share it on your social profiles. Submit it to mining publications or forums. If it's good, it'll get shared."

"What about making money from it?" Sunil asked. "Isn't giving away knowledge for free counterproductive if I want to consult?"

Dusan shook his head. "Common misconception. The free content demonstrates your expertise and builds trust. It brings people to you. The consulting is where they pay for personalized application of that knowledge to their specific situation."

A waiter came by to check on them and refill their water glasses. Through the windows, they could see the lights of a boat moving slowly along the Vltava River.

"Speaking of demonstrating expertise," Dusan continued after the waiter left, "conferences and events are another key channel."

"Like speaking at them?" Sunil looked sceptical. "That seems like a big step."

"You'd be surprised how accessible it is," Dusan replied. "Start small. Local meetups, online webinars, panel discussions where you're not the only expert. Build up to the bigger stages."

"I've never really done public speaking," Sunil admitted.

"Neither had I before mining," Dusan smiled. "My first talk was a ten minute presentation at a tiny Prague Bitcoin meetup with maybe fifteen people. I was terrified. Now I speak at major conferences several times a year."

He pulled out his phone again and showed Sunil a photo of himself on stage at what looked like a large event. "Panel discussion on mining facility design. Great for credibility, amazing for client connections."

Their plates were cleared, and they ordered coffee and dessert. The restaurant had dimmed the lights slightly, making the view of Prague even more spectacular, the city twinkling below them.

"It all seems doable when you break it down like this," Sunil said, looking out at the view. "But it also sounds like a lot of work alongside actually learning the technical stuff."

"It is work," Dusan nodded. "But it compounds over time. Those first blog posts or tweets might not get much traction. But a year of consistent contribution to the community builds something valuable."

"And the mining community? Are they receptive to newcomers?"

"More than most industries, honestly," Dusan said. "Mining is still evolving, still figuring itself out. Fresh perspectives are valued, especially from people with real world experience in related fields."

Their desserts arrived, some kind of traditional Czech cake with a modern presentation. Sunil took a bite and nodded appreciatively.

"One last question," he said. "How do you balance sharing knowledge with keeping proprietary insights for paying clients?"

"Good question," Dusan replied. "Generally, I share methodologies and frameworks openly. The 'what' and 'why' of mining best practices. The specific 'how' tailored to individual situations becomes the consulting work."

"For example, I might publicly share a guide about criteria for selecting mining locations. But the detailed analysis of specific locations for a client's unique needs would be paid work."

They finished their desserts in comfortable silence, looking out at the Prague skyline. Sunil found himself mentally reviewing not just this conversation, but everything he'd learned over the past five days. From the technical basics of Bitcoin mining to business models, energy markets, and now building a professional presence. It was a lot to absorb, but also exciting.

"I need to think about all this," Sunil finally said. "Figure out if it's really a path I want to pursue."

"Of course," Dusan nodded. "No rush. The mining world isn't going anywhere."

"But if I do decide to go for it," Sunil continued, "I might have more questions down the road. Would you mind if I reached out?"

"That's what the mining community is all about," Dusan smiled. "We help each other figure this stuff out. I'd be happy to point you in the right direction as you go along."

After settling the bill, they stepped out onto the restaurant's rooftop terrace for one last look at Prague by night. The air was cool but not cold, perfect for a final moment of reflection.

"Thanks for all this," Sunil said, gesturing broadly at the city below. "What started as a casual invitation turned into quite an education."

"My pleasure," Dusan replied. "Sometimes the best journeys are the unexpected ones."

The next morning came too quickly. Sunil's flight was at noon, and a taxi was scheduled to pick him up at 9 AM. Dusan came to the hotel to see him off, bringing a small bag of Czech souvenirs and snacks for the flight.

"For the journey," he said, handing over the bag. "And this."

He gave Sunil a USB drive. "Some resources to get you started if you decide to pursue mining. E books, guides, templates, contact info for some good people in the industry."

"Thanks," Sunil said, genuinely touched by the gesture. "For everything."

As the taxi pulled away from the hotel, Sunil watched Prague slide past the window. The medieval towers and spires, the winding cobblestone streets, the river with its bridges. A beautiful old city that had unexpectedly opened the door to a possible new future.

Whether he'd walk through that door remained to be seen. But as the taxi headed toward the airport, Sunil was already mentally drafting ideas for his first mining related LinkedIn post.

CHAPTER 21
MINER MANAGEMENT SOFTWARES & BITCOIN LENDING

The taxi pulled up to Václav Havel Airport Prague just after 10 AM, giving Sunil plenty of time for his noon flight. He thanked the driver in his basic Czech, grabbed his luggage, and headed into the departures terminal. The check-in process was smooth, and he made it through security with time to spare.

At the gate, however, his good timing came to an abrupt halt. A digital display showed his flight was delayed by two and a half hours due to air traffic control issues in London. Sunil sighed and looked around the crowded departure area. At least Prague had a decent airport lounge.

He found the business lounge, flashed his credit card for day access, and settled into a comfortable chair near the windows overlooking the tarmac. After ordering a coffee and grabbing some pastries from the buffet, he pulled out his phone and noticed a message from Dusan.

"Safe travels! Let me know when you land. Also remembered something we didn't discuss - hosting management software and Bitcoin lending options. Could be relevant for your consultancy angles."

Sunil glanced at his phone's clock. The delay meant he had time to kill, and his curiosity was piqued. He called Dusan back.

"Flight delayed?" Dusan answered on the second ring.

"Two and a half hours," Sunil groaned. "Air traffic problems. But your timing is perfect. What's this about hosting management and Bitcoin lending?"

"Ah, you've got time then. Perfect." Sunil could hear the smile in Dusan's voice. "These are two areas we barely touched on, but they're becoming huge in the mining world. Both could be interesting angles for your consultancy work."

Sunil settled back in his chair, watching planes taxi past the window. "I'm all ears. Start with the hosting management thing."

"Right, so you know how hosting providers work - they rent space, power, and cooling for miners' equipment. But the business side is incredibly complex. Billing for electricity usage, managing multiple customers, tracking equipment performance, handling customer service..."

"Sounds like a nightmare to manage manually."

"Exactly. That's where miner management software comes in. There are really two categories of solutions that work together - business management platforms like MeasureX, and technical optimisation platforms like Hive OS. Think of them as the complete operating system for mining businesses."

A family with young children settled into chairs nearby, the kids immediately glued to tablets. Sunil adjusted his position to focus on the call.

"How do they work together?" he asked.

"Let me start with MeasureX since that handles the business side. It's basically a comprehensive management platform that automates everything customer-facing. The big innovation is daily electricity payments instead of monthly bills. But here's the clever part -

customers pay up credit in advance, and then that credit gets deducted daily based on their actual power usage."

"Daily payments? That's interesting."

"Yeah, instead of hosting providers having to float massive electricity costs for a month waiting for customer payments, they get paid daily through this credit system. Customers top up their account balance, and it automatically deducts each day. Removes huge financial risk and improves liquidity for the hosting company."

Sunil took a sip of his coffee, thinking about the implications. "And customers are OK with this prepaid approach?"

"More than OK. They prefer it because it gives them better visibility into their actual costs. No surprise bills at the end of the month. Plus they can see their credit balance decreasing in real time, so they know exactly when to top up. The whole system is transparent - customers can see exactly what they're being charged for daily."

"What else does MeasureX handle?"

"Pretty much everything on the business side. Automated customer onboarding where new clients can sign up and start mining directly from the provider's website. Performance monitoring for all the equipment. Billing management that handles complex consumption calculations automatically. Customer dashboards where people can manage their hardware and order new equipment."

A gate announcement echoed through the lounge, but it wasn't for Sunil's flight. He glanced at the departure board - still showing the same delay.

"That does sound comprehensive," he said. "What about the technical side? That's where Hive OS comes in?"

"Exactly. While MeasureX handles customers, billing, and business operations, Hive OS manages the actual mining hardware. But calling it just 'technical optimisation' doesn't do it justice - it's really a complete ecosystem for cryptocurrency mining operations."

"How comprehensive are we talking?"

"Hive OS actually has multiple components working together. There's the core Hive OS operating system, but also Hiveon Enterprise for industrial operations, Hiveon Energy for sustainable solutions, and custom ASIC firmware. It's like having four different tools that all integrate perfectly."

"Can you break that down?"

"Sure. Let's start with the core Hive OS - it's a Linux-based operating system that gives you a unified dashboard to monitor ASIC, GPU, CPU, and FPGA miners in real time across global locations. They're managing over 5 million ASICs globally through this single interface."

"5 million? That's massive."

"Huge scale. But here's where it gets really interesting - their custom ASIC firmware. They replace the stock software on miners like Antminer S19s or Whatsminer M30S units. Can boost hashrate by up to 37% through voltage and frequency optimisation while actually reducing power consumption by 15% to 30%."

"Wait, higher performance and lower power consumption?"

"Exactly. It's all about chip-level tuning and power optimisation. Plus their firmware supports immersion cooling setups by disabling fan checks for liquid-cooled environments."

"And how does the interface work?"

"They call them 'flight sheets' - preconfigured settings for pools, wallets, and mining software that you can deploy instantly. Plus bulk actions so you can update firmware, reboot devices, or adjust overclocking profiles across thousands of ASICs simultaneously."

"Thousands at once?"

"The scalability is incredible. But then there's Hiveon Enterprise, which is their business-grade platform for industrial-scale operations. This is where it gets really sophisticated."

A barista announced fresh coffee at the buffet, and several lounge patrons got up to refresh their drinks. Sunil stayed put, absorbed in the conversation.

"What makes the enterprise version different?"

"Several key components. First is advanced power management - real-time load balancing, demand response integration, and energy cost analytics. They can automatically reduce energy usage when electricity prices exceed set thresholds, helping avoid peak rates."

"That's smart for protecting margins."

"Very smart. I know of a case study where their price response automations lowered the average cost of power by 8% for a site in Buffalo. But there's more - they have complex automation tools."

"Such as?"

"Custom or pre-built workflows to automate everything from price response to firmware updates, reporting, team management, event-based triggers. Plus they've got this Hiveon AI Assistant for operational and revenue optimisation recommendations."

"AI for mining optimisation?"

"The AI helps with seamless business data filtering within the system. Then there's their warehouse module - tracks ASIC lifecycle across different locations from procurement to decommissioning. Very useful for large operations managing equipment across multiple sites."

"And for maintenance?"

"They have a ticketing system that's like a task management tool for technicians to streamline workflow, and for managers to track team efficiency. Everything integrated into one platform."

"This is getting quite complex. What about the energy side you mentioned?"

"Ah, Hiveon Energy - that's their sustainable energy solutions. They do BESS integration, which provides new revenue streams by utilising existing infrastructure. Plus waste methane conversion - repurposing methane emissions for mining operations."

"Methane to mining?"

"Yeah, and renewable integration where they shift mining loads to renewable sources during off-peak hours. Very forward-thinking on the ESG side."

"And for troubleshooting?"

"Remote access capabilities - you can troubleshoot via SSH or their Tele console feature without physical access. Essential when you've got miners spread across multiple locations or countries."

"Security must be important at this scale."

"They're SOC-2 and ISO 27001 certified. When you're managing millions of ASICs worth billions in equipment, security is paramount."

"What about practical benefits for consultants?"

"Several major areas. Operational efficiency is huge - consultants use Hiveon's dashboard to audit farm performance, identify optimisation opportunities and underperforming devices, automate time-consuming operations. I know one case where automated client management saved 380 hours annually for a 15MW farm in Arkansas."

"380 hours saved?"

"Just through automation. But the cost reduction benefits are even more impressive. Beyond the power optimisation I mentioned, their business data analytics are incredibly detailed. Consultants can create custom analytic dashboards to work with large-scale, highly granular business data directly from Hiveon Enterprise."

"Without separate BI systems?"

"Exactly. No need for external business intelligence tools. There's a case study where they recovered $22,000 using stored data to refute a supposedly missed curtailment. Having that level of detailed, audit-ready data is invaluable."

"And for client reporting?"

"Hiveon Enterprise's business reporting module lets you generate customised reports on ROI, uptime, consumption, and equipment profit across different farms and clients. Critical for consultants managing multiple client relationships."

"How do MeasureX and Hive OS work together?"

"Perfect synergy. MeasureX handles the customer-facing business operations while Hive OS optimises the technical performance. Imagine a hosting provider using both - MeasureX automatically bills customers for daily electricity usage while Hive OS's AI optimises power consumption in real time."

"So customers get charged for optimised usage?"

"Exactly. Hive OS might reduce a customer's power consumption by 20% through firmware optimisation, MeasureX automatically adjusts their daily billing to reflect the actual lower usage. Customer saves money, hosting provider maintains margins, equipment runs more efficiently."

"What about the differences between them? They must have different focuses."

"Absolutely. MeasureX is designed specifically for hosting providers and their customers. Strong e-commerce features for hardware sales, CRM systems, intelligent upselling tools, white-labelled dashboards so providers can present their own brand."

"White-labelled?"

"The hosting provider's customers see the provider's branding, not MeasureX. Makes it look like the provider built their own sophisticated platform. Plus MeasureX handles inventory tracking, automated service reports, spare part management, after sales automation."

"And Hive OS focuses more on..."

"Technical optimisation and enterprise-scale operations. Their warehouse module for equipment lifecycle management from procurement to decommissioning. Site maps, ticketing systems for maintenance, 24/7 expert support, plus all the advanced energy management features."

"But they both handle similar basic functions?"

"The fundamentals, yes. Both offer centralised dashboards, remote monitoring and control, automation, real-time power tracking, alerts and notifications, mobile apps, multi-user access. But their strengths are complementary."

"How so?"

"MeasureX excels at customer onboarding, daily electricity billing, contract management, marketplace features where customers can buy or rent miners. Hive OS excels at ASIC firmware optimisation, AI-driven power management, load shifting, renewable energy integration."

"Load shifting again?"

"Hive OS's AI analyses electricity prices and automatically adjusts mining loads to optimise costs. They even have waste methane conversion initiatives - repurposing methane emissions for mining operations. Advanced stuff."

"And profitability tools?"

"Hive OS has built-in mining calculators for real-time earnings and profitability analysis. MeasureX focuses more on cost transparency and billing accuracy rather than profit calculations."

"You mentioned this could be relevant for consultancy work?"

"Absolutely. Think about it from your maritime background. You understand complex logistics, equipment management, customer service operations. Hosting providers face similar challenges - managing physical assets, optimising operations, serving demanding customers. But now they need to do it with both business efficiency and technical optimisation."

"I can see the parallels."

"Plus, as these management platforms become more sophisticated, there's growing demand for consultants who understand both the technical mining side and the business operations side. Providers need help choosing between solutions like MeasureX and Hive OS, or figuring out how to implement both effectively."

"Do most providers use both?"

"The smart ones do. MeasureX handles customer relationships and billing automation, Hive OS handles technical performance and equipment optimisation. Together they create a complete solution that traditional hosting providers can't match."

"What about implementation complexity?"

"That's where consultants add real value. Installing Hive OS firmware requires technical expertise - you're flashing custom software onto expensive ASIC miners. MeasureX implementation involves integrating with existing business systems, training customer service teams, migrating billing processes."

"Sounds like plenty of room for things to go wrong."

"Exactly. I know consultants who specialise in helping hosting providers implement these platforms properly. They might charge $50,000 to $100,000 for a complete implementation project, but they save providers months of trial and error."

"And the results?"

"Dramatic. I mentioned earlier about a 10 megawatt farm reducing electricity costs by using Hive OS's energy optimisation. But combine that with MeasureX's daily billing automation, and you're talking about complete transformation of the business model."

"How so?"

"Traditional hosting providers operate on monthly billing cycles, manual customer service, basic equipment monitoring. They're constantly dealing with cash flow issues, billing disputes, equipment downtime they don't detect until customers complain."

"And with both platforms?"

"Daily payments solve cash flow problems immediately. Automated customer onboarding and billing eliminate most manual work. Predictive maintenance prevents equipment failures before they happen. Customer satisfaction goes up, operational costs go down, margins improve significantly."

"That's quite a value proposition."

"It has to be. The hosting business is getting more competitive, so providers need every advantage they can get. Better customer experience, lower operational costs, improved cash flow, technical optimisation - platforms like MeasureX and Hive OS deliver all of that."

"And this is becoming standard in the industry?"

"Rapidly. The providers who don't adopt these tools are getting left behind. Customers expect real-time visibility, automated billing, technical optimisation. If you can't provide that, they'll find someone who can."

"You mentioned this could be relevant for consultancy work?"

"Absolutely. Think about it from your maritime background. You understand complex logistics, equipment management, customer service operations. Hosting providers face similar challenges - managing physical assets, optimising operations, serving demanding customers."

"I can see the parallels."

"Plus, as these management platforms become more sophisticated, there's growing demand for consultants who understand both the technical mining side and the business operations side. Providers need help choosing the right systems, implementing them properly, optimising their use."

"Interesting angle," Sunil mused. "What about this Bitcoin lending thing you mentioned?"

"Ah, that's a whole other world." Dusan's tone became more serious. "Bitcoin lending is becoming huge for miners, especially larger operations. Basically using Bitcoin or mining equipment as collateral for loans."

"Why would miners need loans if they're earning bitcoin?"

"Several reasons. Maybe they want to expand operations but don't want to sell their bitcoin to buy new equipment. Maybe they need working capital for electricity and operational costs while holding their bitcoin long term. Or maybe they want to hedge against bitcoin price volatility."

A couple at a nearby table was having an animated discussion in what sounded like German about their connecting flight. Sunil turned slightly away to focus on Dusan's explanation.

"How does it work practically?"

"Depends on the setup. Some platforms let you borrow against your Bitcoin holdings - you put up Bitcoin as collateral and get a loan in dollars or stablecoins. Other platforms let you borrow against your mining equipment or future mining revenues."

"And the interest rates?"

"Varies widely based on collateral, loan terms, and market conditions. Could be anywhere from 5% to 15% annually. Usually much better than traditional business loans, especially for newer mining operations that banks don't understand."

"What are the risks?"

"Main risk is liquidation. If bitcoin price drops significantly, your collateral might not cover the loan anymore. The lender can liquidate your Bitcoin to repay the debt. Some platforms have margin calls where you need to add more collateral if the ratio gets too low."

Sunil watched a large aircraft push back from a gate, its engines starting with visible heat shimmer. "Sounds risky for volatile markets."

"It can be. But for experienced miners, it's a useful tool. Let's say you've got 10 bitcoin from mining over the past year. Instead of selling 5 bitcoin to buy new equipment, you could borrow against all 10 and keep your long term Bitcoin position."

"Assuming bitcoin price goes up."

"Right. If Bitcoin appreciates significantly, you win twice - your collateral is worth more, plus you didn't have to sell any to fund expansion. But if it crashes, you could lose everything."

The lounge was getting busier as more delayed flights filled up with frustrated travellers. Sunil checked his phone - still another hour and a half until his revised departure time.

"Are there different types of Bitcoin lending?"

"There are really two main categories. DeFi lending and institutional lending. Each works completely differently."

"DeFi?"

"Decentralised Finance. Platforms like Compound or Aave that use smart contracts instead of traditional banks. You connect directly with lenders through these protocols, no middleman needed."

"How does that work exactly?"

"Take Compound, for example. You can borrow against Bitcoin collateral and get a loan in dollars or stablecoins. The whole thing is managed by smart contracts and automated market mechanisms."

Sunil shifted in his chair, intrigued. "What kind of terms?"

"Here's where it gets interesting - everything is variable. LTV is usually around 70% to 80%, though you can choose a lower LTV if you want extra safety. Interest rates can be as low as 3% to 4% or as high as 12%, depending on market conditions."

"Why is everything variable? That seems unpredictable."

"Great question," came the reply. "DeFi borrowing terms are variable because interest rates are determined by real-time supply and demand dynamics, not by a central authority. It's all about automated market balancing."

"How does that work?"

"Platforms like Compound use smart contracts to adjust borrowing rates automatically. When demand for loans increases or the supply of available assets decreases, interest rates rise to attract more lenders. When there's excess supply or low borrowing demand, rates decrease to encourage borrowing."

"So it's like a live auction?"

"Exactly. The core mechanism is the utilisation rate - the ratio of borrowed funds to total supplied funds. Interest rates are set as a direct function of this utilisation rate, so they change constantly as users deposit, withdraw, or borrow."

A coffee cup clinked somewhere nearby as Sunil processed this. "What's LTV exactly?"

"Loan-to-Value ratio. It's basically how much you can borrow against your collateral. If you have $100 worth of bitcoin and the LTV is 75%, you can borrow up to $75. It's the most important number in any lending arrangement."

"And liquidation?"

"That's when things get serious. The liquidation factor is the point at which your collateral gets automatically sold to repay the debt. Sometimes it's the same as your LTV, sometimes it's 5% above. If bitcoin's price drops and your loan amount approaches this threshold, the smart contract liquidates your collateral."

"What about penalties?"

"Liquidation penalty is also variable - can be 5% or more. The beauty of DeFi is this flexibility, but it also means you need to watch market conditions carefully."

"And the platform doesn't touch your Bitcoin?"

"In true DeFi like Compound, your Bitcoin gets locked in smart contracts, not controlled by any company. No rehypothecation, meaning they can't lend out your collateral to someone else. It stays locked until you repay."

"Why all this variability instead of fixed terms?"

"Three main reasons. First, it's risk management - variable rates help manage risk by responding to market volatility. If protocols locked in fixed rates but market conditions changed dramatically, they could face insolvency."

"Second, it's pure decentralisation. Without a central authority, DeFi relies on transparent, algorithmic models encoded in smart contracts. They operate autonomously based on real market activity."

"And third, it gives users flexibility to enter and exit loans anytime, with rates reflecting current market realities. You're not locked into terms that might become unfavourable."

"And institutional lending?"

"That's the traditional route - global investment firms that specialise in asset-backed financing. Much larger scale, different risk models."

"How different?"

"Four main custody models. First is hypothecation - you pledge Bitcoin as collateral but keep ownership. Lender holds it as security but can't use it unless you default."

"Makes sense."

"Then there's rehypothecation - lender can actually use your collateral for their own purposes, like securing their own borrowing. Higher risk but sometimes better rates."

"They can gamble with my Bitcoin?"

"If you agree to it, yes. That's how some platforms like Celsius got in trouble - they were rehypothecating customer funds for risky investments."

"What are the other models?"

"Segregated custody means your collateral is kept completely separate, never mixed with other assets. And non-rehypothecation is a contractual promise that they won't use your collateral, period."

The lounge announcer called another flight, and Sunil checked his phone again. Still time before boarding.

"What about terms for institutional lending?"

"Much longer timeframes - minimum one to three years, renewable after that. Loan-to-value ratios from 60% to 85%, so potentially better than DeFi. Interest rates vary widely though."

"How widely?"

"Could be fixed rates from 2% to 10% depending on collateral amount, loan tenure, and custody model. Or floating rates tied to benchmarks."

"Benchmarks?"

"Like SOFR plus 4% to 4.5%. SOFR is the Secured Overnight Financing Rate - basically the cost of borrowing cash overnight using US Treasury securities as collateral. It replaced LIBOR as the main benchmark."

"So if SOFR is 5.3%, I'd pay..."

"5.3% plus 4.5%, so 9.8% total. The rate adjusts as SOFR changes, which can be good or bad depending on market conditions."

"Sounds like both options have serious trade-offs."

"Exactly. DeFi gives you transparency and real-time market pricing but variable terms and shorter durations. Institutional gives you potentially better rates and longer terms but more counterparty risk and complexity."

A gate agent made an announcement about boarding for a flight to Munich. Sunil glanced over, then refocused on the call.

"What about more direct lending arrangements?"

"Yeah, there's also peer to peer lending where you might lend directly to other miners or businesses, using smart contracts or escrow services. Higher potential returns but also higher risk since you're essentially becoming a private lender."

"And equipment financing?"

"That's becoming big too. Instead of borrowing against Bitcoin, you borrow against the mining equipment itself. The lender technically owns the equipment until you pay off the loan. Less volatile than Bitcoin collateral since ASIC values are more predictable."

"Though they do depreciate pretty fast," Sunil pointed out.

"True. But the cash flows are more predictable too. A lender can calculate expected mining revenues pretty accurately and structure the loan around that. Some platforms even automate the entire process - you apply online, they assess your mining setup and projected earnings, approve the loan digitally."

Sunil finished his coffee and considered getting another. "Where does the lending capital come from?"

"Mix of sources. Some platforms raise traditional investment capital. Others aggregate deposits from Bitcoin holders looking for yield. Some partner with traditional banks or credit funds that want exposure to Bitcoin mining."

"And this ties into hosting how?"

"Good question. Some hosting providers are getting into lending as an additional service. They already understand their customers' operations, equipment values, performance metrics. Natural extension to offer financing for equipment purchases or operational capital."

"Plus they could work with management platforms like MeasureX to automate the whole process?"

"Exactly. Imagine a hosting customer wants to expand their operation. They could apply for equipment financing directly through their MeasureX dashboard. The platform already has all their performance data, payment history, operational metrics. Could make lending decisions much faster and more accurately than traditional lenders."

A janitor wheeled a cart past Sunil's table, efficiently clearing and wiping down surfaces. The lounge maintained its calm atmosphere despite the growing crowd.

"This is getting quite complex," Sunil said. "Hosting management, Bitcoin lending, equipment financing... it's like a whole financial ecosystem around mining."

"That's exactly what it is. And it's evolving rapidly. Traditional financial services are starting to understand mining as a legitimate business. Specialized fintech companies are building products specifically for miners. Insurance companies are offering coverage for mining operations."

"Insurance?"

"Yeah, coverage for equipment, business interruption, even cyber-attacks. Some policies cover lost revenues if your hosting provider has problems or if pool pay outs are delayed."

"Makes sense given how much capital is involved."

"Right. A large mining operation might have millions in equipment, hundreds of thousands in monthly electricity costs, complex contracts with hosting providers and power companies. Managing all that financial complexity requires sophisticated tools."

Sunil checked the departure board again. His flight was now showing "Boarding Soon" which seemed optimistic given the earlier delay estimate.

"So from a consultancy perspective, this represents another potential specialisation area?"

"Definitely. Mining operations consulting is becoming its own field, but it's really three specialisations rolled into one. Business operations consulting around platforms like MeasureX, technical optimisation consulting around platforms like Hive OS, and mining finance consulting around lending and capital structure."

"And the operational side too, with tools like both platforms working together?"

"Absolutely. Consultants are using the combined data from both platforms to provide unprecedented insights. I know one consultant who helped a 50 megawatt farm reduce total operational costs by 35% using integrated analytics from MeasureX and Hive OS."

"How?"

"MeasureX identified that certain customers were consistently late on payments despite good mining performance. Hive OS data showed their equipment was actually overperforming compared to others. Investigation revealed they were sophisticated operators mining the most profitable altcoins and needed different billing structures."

"So the solution was?"

"Flexible billing options through MeasureX that better matched their actual revenue cycles, plus premium hosting rates for the extra management complexity. Customer retention improved, margins increased, and the hosting provider learned to target similar sophisticated customers."

"That's quite sophisticated analysis."

"It has to be. Modern mining operations need business intelligence that spans customer behaviour, technical performance, financial optimisation, and market dynamics. The platforms provide raw data, but extracting actionable insights requires expertise across multiple domains."

"What about the learning resources? Where would someone start?"

"For the technical side, both platforms have extensive documentation. Hive OS offers training courses on firmware optimisation, chip-level tuning, cooling system integration. MeasureX has business process workshops covering billing automation, customer experience optimisation, marketplace management."

"Hands-on experience?"

"Critical. Start small - maybe help a friend implement MeasureX for their hosting business, or optimise a few ASICs with Hive OS firmware. The learning curve is steep but the platforms are designed to reduce complexity over time."

"And for Bitcoin lending?"

"Start with the educational resources from major platforms, but also study the failures like Celsius to understand risk management. Try small amounts on DeFi platforms to understand user experience.

Most importantly, talk to actual miners about their capital needs and financing challenges."

"Any specific resources?"

"Digital Mining Solutions by Nico Smid publishes good research on industry trends including financing and technical developments. Hive OS and MeasureX both publish case studies and implementation guides. And there are several mining technology conferences where you can meet people working with these platforms."

"What about the integration challenges? It sounds like getting everything working together properly could be complex."

"Very complex. Each platform has its own data formats, APIs, user management systems. Getting MeasureX billing to automatically adjust based on Hive OS performance data requires custom integration work. Most hosting providers don't have the technical expertise in-house."

"So consultants who understand both platforms..."

"Are in high demand. The providers who can offer both business efficiency and technical optimisation have significant competitive advantages. But implementing both platforms properly requires expertise in business process redesign, technical system integration, change management, and ongoing optimisation."

"And this market is growing?"

"Rapidly. Traditional hosting providers are realising they need to evolve or get displaced by tech-savvy competitors. New entrants are building their businesses around these platforms from day one. The hosting industry is going through the same transformation that many industries have experienced - manual processes being replaced by automated, data-driven operations."

"With similar opportunities for consultants who understand the transition?"

"Exactly. Plus the international aspect - these platforms are being adopted globally, but implementation challenges vary by region. Power market structures, regulatory requirements, customer expectations all differ. Local expertise combined with platform knowledge is incredibly valuable."

A gate agent announced that Sunil's flight was beginning boarding. He gathered his belongings while continuing the conversation.

"One last question. If someone wanted to learn more about these topics, where would you suggest starting?"

"For hosting management, I'd recommend talking to actual hosting providers about their operational challenges. Many are happy to discuss their pain points. For technical optimisation, start with Hive OS's documentation and try to get hands-on experience with ASIC firmware. For Bitcoin lending, start with the major platforms' educational resources, but also read about the failures like Celsius to understand what can go wrong."

"Any specific starting points?"

"Download the free versions of both platforms and explore their interfaces. MeasureX offers demos of their customer onboarding and billing workflows. Hive OS has simulators for their firmware optimisation tools. Understanding the user experience is crucial for consultancy work."

"And for staying current?"

"Follow the platforms' development roadmaps. Both MeasureX and Hive OS are rapidly adding features - AI-driven insights, advanced automation, better integration capabilities. The consultants who understand the latest features have competitive advantages."

"What about networking?"

"Mining industry meetups, hosting provider associations, fintech conferences focused on crypto lending. The community is surprisingly collaborative - people share challenges and solutions openly. Plus many consultants specialise in specific aspects and refer work to each other."

Sunil stood up and shouldered his carry-on bag. "This has been incredibly helpful. Gives me a lot to think about during the flight."

"My pleasure. And seriously, if you decide to pursue any of these angles, the industry needs more people who understand the intersection of business operations, technical optimisation, and financial strategy. Most consultants are strong in one area but weak in the others. Someone who can help with pool selection, platform implementation, lending strategy, and ongoing optimisation would be incredibly valuable."

"I'll definitely do more research when I get home. Thanks for taking the time to explain all this."

"Of course. Safe travels, and let me know how your thinking evolves. This stuff changes fast, so staying current is important. New platform features launch regularly, lending products evolve constantly, hosting business models keep improving."

As Sunil headed toward his gate, his mind was already processing everything he'd learned. The conversation had revealed yet another layer of complexity in the Bitcoin mining world. What had started as a simple discussion about computer hardware had evolved into a comprehensive view of an entire industry ecosystem - technical, operational, and financial.

He joined the boarding queue, pulling out his phone to make some quick notes about the key points while they were fresh in his memory. MeasureX for hosting automation and customer management, Hive OS for technical optimisation and firmware enhancement, DeFi vs institutional Bitcoin lending models, equipment financing options, insurance considerations, integration challenges and opportunities. Each represented potential areas for deeper learning and possible consultancy specialisation.

The technical integration possibilities fascinated him most. MeasureX handling customer relationships and automated billing, Hive OS optimising hardware performance and predicting maintenance needs, lending platforms providing growth capital with data-driven decisions, all working together in a sophisticated ecosystem that barely existed five years ago.

What struck him was how the maritime industry had undergone similar transformations - manual processes replaced by automated systems, data-driven decision making, integrated platforms managing everything from logistics to financial settlements. His background might be more relevant than he'd initially thought.

As he settled into his airplane seat twenty minutes later, Sunil realised that his week in Prague had given him far more than just an introduction to Bitcoin mining. It had opened his eyes to an entire new industry that intersected with many of his existing skills and interests. Whether he ultimately pursued mining consultancy or not, the knowledge would be valuable.

The plane pushed back from the gate, finally beginning its journey to London. Sunil looked out the window at Prague's skyline one last time, already planning his next steps for learning about this fascinating and complex world Dusan had introduced him to. The USB drive of resources in his bag would be just the beginning, but now he had a much clearer sense of where to focus his research efforts.

The integration of business management, technical optimisation, and financial services in mining was creating opportunities that reminded him of the early days of maritime logistics automation. Those who understood the intersection of multiple domains had thrived during that transition. Perhaps the same would be true in Bitcoin mining.

EPILOGUE

So here we are, at the end of our journey together. When we started, we talked about Bitcoin being like digital gold, this revolutionary thing changing how we think about money. We used to compare it to Tesla and SpaceX. Game changers that reshape industries. After everything we've covered about mining, we hope you now see why even those comparisons don't quite capture what Bitcoin really is.

We've come a long way, haven't we? From those first conversations about blockchain basics to digging into the nitty gritty of ASIC miners, cooling systems, and energy markets across the world. What began as me sharing a meal with Dusan in Prague somehow turned into this roadmap for anyone wanting to get into the mining world.

I mentioned at the start that Bitcoin often seems attractive but lacks clear instructions on how to actually get involved. That's the gap I wanted to fill. Not with theory or technical jargon that puts people to sleep, but with real stuff I learned through experience, through mistakes, through conversations with people who've been in the trenches. Whether you're thinking about setting up one miner in your garage or building a consulting business, you've now got a foundation to build on.

Look, mining isn't just about making money. Sure, that's a big part of it for most of us, let's be honest. But it's also about being part of something bigger. When you mine Bitcoin, you're not just running some computer program. You're helping maintain this system that exists outside the control of governments and banks. You're supporting a financial network that can't be shut down or censored. That's pretty cool when you think about it.

I'm not going to sugar-coat it though. Mining has gotten tough. Remember when people mined Bitcoin on laptops? Those days are long gone. Now it's an industry with serious players, specialized equipment, and razor thin margins. The competition is brutal, the market swings wildly, and the technical challenges just keep coming.

But for folks willing to put in the work, opportunities are still out there. Maybe it's finding cheap power in some corner of the world. Maybe it's turning your knowledge into consulting gigs. Maybe it's solving problems nobody else has figured out yet. The industry keeps changing, and change always brings new chances to carve out your spot.

One thing I really hope you've picked up on is how mining impacts more than just Bitcoin markets. We talked about using wasted energy, balancing power grids, repurposing heat, even supporting green energy development. That stuff rarely makes headlines, but to me, it's some of the most interesting aspects of what mining can do.

What's coming next? Energy efficiency will keep improving. Mining and energy markets will become more intertwined. Governments will create new rules, some helpful, some not. And gradually, the economics will shift from block rewards to transaction fees. Miners who see these changes coming and adapt will be the ones who thrive.

For those of you thinking about consulting, remember that your value isn't just what you know about mining. It's how well you can explain complicated stuff to people who don't get it. It's your ability to give practical advice, not just theory. Clear explanations and useful guidance are rare skills, and people pay good money for them.

When I first thought about writing this, I wanted to create the book I wish someone had handed me when I was starting out. Not just how to connect wires and run software, but why mining matters and where it might be headed. Something practical that acknowledges the hard parts without getting bogged down in them.

I hope you found what you were looking for in these pages. Maybe you're just curious about how Bitcoin works. Maybe you're seriously thinking about mining as a business. Maybe you want to use what you know to help others. Whatever brought you here, I hope you found some value.

Bitcoin came out of the 2008 financial mess as this alternative vision for how money could work. Instead of trusting institutions, we could trust math and code. More than a decade later, it's proven tougher and more adaptable than most people expected. Pretty amazing to be part of that story, even as just an observer.

Remember I said Bitcoin gives control back to regular people? After everything we've covered, I hope that makes more sense now. Mining isn't just about creating new coins. It's about securing and supporting this whole new financial system. Being part of something that could actually change how the world works.

Will technology keep evolving? Of course. New problems will pop up. Old problems will morph into different ones. But the core idea of Bitcoin mining stays the same: you're helping run a financial network that anyone can use and no one controls.

Thanks for sticking with us through all this. Whether you become a miner, a consultant, or just someone who understands what all the fuss is about, you now know stuff that most people don't. Use that knowledge well, keep learning, and remember that in Bitcoin, standing still means falling behind.

This isn't really the end, you know. In a way, it's just the beginning of whatever comes next for you in this space. Whatever path you choose, we wish you good luck, cheap electricity, and plenty of profitable blocks.

- **Sunil Kumar & Dusan Matuska**

www.ingramcontent.com/pod-product-compliance
Ingram Content Group UK Ltd.
Pitfield, Milton Keynes, MK11 3LW, UK
UKHW021411190726
13845UKWH00028B/1020

9 788198 870605